DATE DUE

MAR 9 1990			
MAY 2 4 1991			
JUN 2 1992			
JUN 4 1993			
NOV 17 1993			
DEC 1 1 1993			
NOV 3 1 1993			
MAR 1 1			

HIGHSMITH 45-220

S P A C E

BATTLEGROUND OF THE FUTURE?

S P A C E
BATTLEGROUND OF THE FUTURE?

BY L.B. TAYLOR, JR.

Franklin Watts
New York/London/Toronto/Sydney/1988
An Impact Book, Revised Edition

Cover photograph by
Los Alamos National Laboratory

Illustrations by Vantage Art, Inc.

Photographs courtesy of:
Department of Defense: pp. 27, 35, 41,
45, 74 (top); U.S. Army: pp. 44, 115;
U.S. Air Force: pp. 63, 68, 74 (bottom);
NASA: p. 120

Library of Congress Cataloging-in-Publication Data
Taylor, L. B.
Space: battleground of the future?
by L.B. Taylor, Jr.—Rev. ed.
p.   cm.—(An Impact book)
Bibliography: p.
Includes index.
Summary: Examines recent developments and trends in
space technology and the arms race which may determine
whether mankind will preserve space for peaceful uses
or turn it into the ultimate battleground.
ISBN 0-531-10514-8
1. Astronautics, Military—Juvenile literature. 2. Space warfare—
Juvenile literature. [1. Astronautics, Military. 2. Space
warfare. 3. War.] I. Title.
UG1520.T39 1988
358'.174—dc19   87-29609 CIP AC

CONTENTS

S P A C E

BATTLEGROUND OF THE FUTURE?

O N E

A MAD POLICY

For the past twenty years or so, the entire world has been sitting on a live, ticking bomb, one that can be set off at any instant with little warning and is capable of destroying our entire planet in a matter of minutes.

The "bomb" is actually the heavily stockpiled nuclear arsenals of the United States and the Soviet Union. Atomic scientists say that, conservatively, the two countries have stored up enough nuclear bomb warheads to effectively blow up the earth several times over.

Yet, incredibly, while this fearsome threat of destruction hangs over our heads on a daily basis—as it has for the past two decades—we have done preciously little to defend ourselves against attack. Instead, what the United States and the Soviet Union have done is to continue to build bigger, better, and smarter offensive bombs.

If all this sounds frightening, it is. The strategy behind such a questionable policy is that if both the United States and the Soviet Union develop enough weapons of destruction, then neither country will strike the other with nuclear arms for fear of massive retaliation. If, for example, the Soviets were to launch a barrage of nuclear-tipped warheads at America, even if they hit on target within thirty minutes, they know that the United States has the capability to return the fire in kind. Tens of millions of Americans might be killed in such an onslaught, but there would be time for retaliation; tens of millions of Russians would also be obliterated, and the land would be scorched to uselessness.

Why, one might reasonably ask, can't an effective defense be built to shield us from nuclear attack? Such a defense, generally called an antiballistic missile system, would cost countless billions of dollars. Even if such a system were in place, it could at best protect only a relatively small percentage of the overall population.

And such a system would constantly have to be upgraded. Each time a new offensive weapon was devised, improvements would have to be made in the defensive system to keep pace. This would lead to an insane, ever-spiraling escalation of more billions of dollars that would have no end.

Realizing this, the United States and Russia agreed, in 1972, to an Antiballistic Missile (ABM) treaty. In part, this said, "Each party (that is, the United States or the USSR) undertakes not to deploy ABM systems for defense of the territory of its country and not to provide a base for such defense."

This committed the United States and Russia to keep their countries undefended against nuclear attack. This way, officials believed, neither side would order a first strike attack on the other, because it could not defend itself in return.

This philosophy came to be known as Mutual Assured Destruction (MAD), because it assures the destruction of both nations if either one makes a mistake. Critics of the idea called it MAD because they feel such a policy was idiotic to start with. This criticism has grown more severe in recent years as the Soviets have continued to develop more missiles, stronger warheads, and more sophisticated weapons. At the same time, the

United States retaliatory strike force has become more vulnerable to enemy attack.

For the past generation, the U.S. concept of security has been based on a strategic nuclear triad. This is a three-pronged nuclear force that has included: land-based intercontinental ballistic missiles housed in hardened silos on the ground; Poseidon and Trident submarines with nuclear missiles at sea; and B-52 bombers in the air. The bombers are being replaced by newer B-1 aircraft and cruise missiles.

The theory of triad was, and still is, that if an enemy could knock out one part of the force—say, if Soviet missiles could destroy U.S. land-based missiles before they could be launched—the other two legs of the triad, the bombers and submarine-based missiles, could be used to strike back. Even if two parts of the triad were wiped out, the United States would still have enough firepower to deter a foreign attack.

But as the Russians have streamlined their offensive missiles, U.S. experts have become more and more worried about the triad strategy. It is now believed that the Russians have the accuracy to demolish all U.S. land-based missiles.

Space expert and author Dr. Robert Jastrow, founder of the Institute for Space Studies, has said that "the Soviet Union has created a massive nuclear stockpile that seems to be designed for the destruction of the United States, rather than as a deterrent to an attack on the USSR."[1] Jastrow says this arsenal includes thousands of nuclear warheads, any one of which can deposit the equivalent of half a million tons of TNT within a 300-yard (274-m) radius of a target.

The Soviet nuclear missile force is estimated to have more than 8,000 accurate nuclear warheads. As Jastrow points out, "With two [warheads] targeted on each of the 4,000 critical U.S. military sites, the Soviets could destroy them all."

And right now, the air wing of the U.S. triad defense is weak because the current bomber force of B-52s is old and may no longer be effective until the newer B-1 bombers are brought into action.

This would leave America with only the sea-based missile force as an effective deterrent, and it is believed the Russians are working hard at devising a system to counter this as well. Jastrow says this could happen as early as the 1990s. He notes that subs churn up a thermal "wake" that can be detected by satellites in space. Submerged submarines also create changes in the "sea-state"—the irregular pattern of waves that continually crosses the ocean surface. According to Jastrow, details of the sea-state can be measured from satellites with a new type of radar. The Russians are working hard on developing such detection systems, and if and when they succeed, the United States will have lost its most important and least vulnerable means of retaliation against a Soviet attack.

Further, there is significant evidence that the Russians have violated the ABM treaty by building an antimissile defense network around Moscow, the Soviet capital. This system consists of several dozen Galosh ABMs with a range of several hundred miles.

It is felt that if the Russians ever thought they could launch a major attack against the United States without fear of being attacked with equal power in return, they might do so. Or, nearly as bad, they could, in effect, hold the United States hostage via nuclear blackmail.

To keep from getting into such an untenable/ position, the United States has been spending record sums of money to beef up its defenses. The annual Department of Defense budget is now well over $300 billion and continues to grow at an alarming pace. The Russians, too, spend a disproportionate percentage of their budget for arms.

Meanwhile, efforts of U.S. and Russian leaders to

find some way to meaningfully reduce this maddening nuclear arms race have not succeeded. Negotiations have gone on for years, but little good has resulted. Neither side trusts the other.

Where will all this lead? Will we continue to spend hundreds of billions of dollars on developing bigger and more deadly weapons systems that often will be rendered obsolete shortly after their deployment? Will we have to live forever with the threat of instant annihilation hanging over our heads? Isn't there some way to come up with some system that is better and more sane than Mutual Assured Destruction?

Quite possibly the answer to all these questions was broadcast to the American people in a now famous speech President Ronald Reagan gave on March 23, 1983.

T W O

A BRIGHT NEW CONCEPT

President Reagan's March 1983 speech to the nation was about national defense, but toward the end of the talk he made reference to a new concept which offered fresh hope for nuclear disarmament. Following are excerpts from his speech:

My predecessors in the Oval Office have appeared before you on other occasions to describe the threat posed by Soviet power and have proposed steps to address that threat. But since the advent of nuclear weapons, those steps have been increasingly directed toward deterrence of aggression through the promise of retaliation. This approach to stability through offensive threat has worked. We and our allies have succeeded in preventing nuclear war for more than three decades.

. . . however . . . my advisors . . . have underscored the necessity to break out of a future that relies solely on offensive retaliation for our security. Over the course of these discussions, I have become more and more deeply convinced that the human spirit must be capable of rising above dealing with other nations and human beings by threatening their existence. Feeling this way, I believe we must thoroughly examine every opportunity for

reducing tensions, and for introducing greater stability . . . on both sides.

One of the most important contributions we can make is, of course, to lower the level of all arms, and particularly nuclear arms. We are engaged right now in several negotiations with the Soviet Union to bring about a mutual reduction of weapons. . . . If the Soviet Union will join with us in our effort to achieve major reduction, we will have succeeded in stabilizing the nuclear balance.

Nevertheless, it will still be necessary to rely on the spectre of retaliation, on mutual threat. And that is a sad commentary on the human condition. Wouldn't it be better to save lives than to avenge them? Are we not capable of demonstrating our peaceful intentions by applying all our abilities and our ingenuity to achieving a truly lasting stability? I think we are. Indeed, we must.

Here, President Reagan began to talk about a bold new plan.

. . . I believe there is a way. Let me share with you a vision of the future which offers hope. It is that we embark on a program to counter the awesome Soviet missile threat with measures that are defensive. Let us turn to the very strengths in technology that spawned our great industrial base, and that have given us the quality of life we enjoy today.

What if free people could live secure in the knowledge that their security did not rest upon the threat of instant U.S. retaliations to deter a Soviet attack, that we could intercept and destroy strategic ballistic missiles before they reached our own soil or that of our allies?

I know this is a formidable technical task, one that may not be accomplished before the end of this century. Yet, current technology has attained a level of sophistication where it is reasonable for us to begin this effort. It will take years, probably decades of effort on many fronts. There will be failures and setbacks, just as there will be successes and breakthroughs. And as we proceed, we must remain constant in preserving the nuclear deterrent and maintaining a solid capability for flexible response.

But isn't it worth every investment necessary to free the world from the threat of nuclear war? We know it is.

. . . I call upon the scientific community in our country, those who gave us nuclear weapons, to turn their great talents now to the cause of mankind and world peace, to give us the means of rendering these nuclear weapons impotent and obsolete.

Tonight, consistent with our obligations of the ABM Treaty and recognizing the need for closer consultation with our allies, I'm taking an important first step. I am directing a comprehensive and intensive effort to define a long-term research and development program to begin to achieve our ultimate goal of eliminating the threat posed by strategic nuclear missiles.

This could pave the way for arms control measures to eliminate the weapons themselves. We seek neither military superiority nor political advantage. Our only purpose—one all people share—is to search for ways to reduce the danger of nuclear war.

My fellow Americans, tonight we're launching an effort which holds the promise of changing the course of human history. There will be risks, and results take time. But I believe we can do it. As we cross this threshold, I ask for your prayers and your support.[2]

With this dramatic speech, President Reagan launched the United States into the era of "Star Wars."

T H R E E

THE STAR WARS PLAN

What was the magic defensive system the president referred to in his address to the nation?

What is "Star Wars"?

Officially, the concept is known as the Strategic Defense Initiative (SDI), although the media popularly refer to it as Star Wars.

While researchers in laboratories and offices across the nation have been working on some elements of SDI for several years, specific elements of the program have changed considerably as new technologies have emerged. It also has been difficult to pinpont a precise definition of SDI, because much of it has been shrouded in secrecy.

But there are some common denominators. Experts agree that to be successful, SDI must be a defensive program that has distinct multiple facets. These are commonly called "layers" of defense, with each layer aimed at destroying enemy intercontinental ballistic missiles (ICBMs) through different technologies and different methods.

The respective layers, probably about three, when deployed, would form a protective shield for the United States against ICBM attack. The concept is that one layer of SDI would be designed to attack enemy missiles just

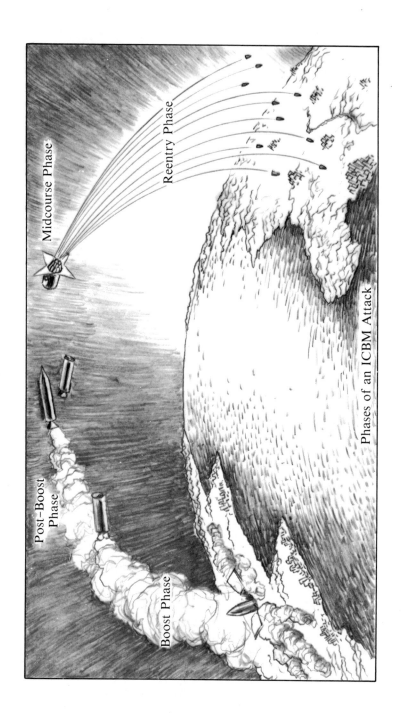

Boost Phase

Post–Boost Phase

Midcourse Phase

Reentry Phase

Phases of an ICBM Attack

as they lift off their launching pads. This is when they are most vulnerable. Burdened by thousands of gallons of fuel, they move upward at an agonizingly slow pace for the first minute or so of flight.

It is especially advantageous to take out an ICBM at this point, too, because most of these missiles carry multiple warheads, as many as ten, and a hit at this point would destroy all the warheads at one time.

The second layer in the shield would be aimed at those ICBMs that escaped being shot down in the launch phase. These would be attacked in space in mid-flight. And the third phase, the so-called last ditch effort, would try to knock out nuclear warheads that had slipped through the first two layers of defense, shortly before they landed on target.

The three layers are needed, SDI proponents say, because it is doubtful that any one layer could knock out all of the thousands of ICBMs that are likely to be launched at one time in the event of a first-strike nuclear attack. It is believed that an effective first layer of defense could destroy up to 80 percent or more of missiles before they escaped the earth's atmosphere after launch. The mid-course layer would take care of most of the surviving missiles and warheads halfway through their flights. And the third layer would zero in on most of the remaining ICBMs before they reached their targets. Overall, say SDI backers, such a three-layered shield could knock down 99 percent of the enemy's missiles.

That would still mean that a few might get through. But the enemy, knowing that a first-strike attack would immediately trigger a massive retaliatory attack, would not be willing to take such a risk.

On paper, such a defensive shield looks great. The big questions are how soon can such a system be developed and how much will it cost? And here, the experts do not agree. Some critics charge that it will take decades, perhaps well into the twenty-first century, before some elements of SDI could be deployed. They say the technological problems are enormous. Proponents of the program say recent technical breakthroughs have greatly shortened the amount of time it would take to put SDI in place, that it conceivably could be done in the 1990s.

Critics contend that it would cost up to $1 trillion to build SDI. Proponents say it could be done for as little as $25 billion. The answers to the time and cost factors probably lie somewhere in between these extremes.

Actually, some elements of SDI could be developed on relatively short notice. For example, the technology for creating the third layer of defense—aimed at knocking down ICBMs shortly before they land on their targets—already exists. However, other elements of the program, such as the first layer, a system to knock down enemy missiles in their launch phase, call for far more exotic weapons, and may take several years of concentrated work to develop.

Following President Reagan's Star Wars speech, a blue ribbon panel of some fifty of the nation's best technical minds was assembled and given the charge to devote its efforts almost exclusively to one problem—the defense against ballistic missiles. The group was chaired by Dr. James Fletcher, the present head of the National Aeronautics and Space Administration (NASA). The team included experts from the aerospace industry, Department of Defense "think tanks," and prestigious research centers.

For five months they considered what it would take to halt an attack by Soviet ICBMs. They analyzed the current U.S. technological base and gave serious thought to what the Russians might do to counter an antimissile system.

The panel concluded that a comprehensive ballistic missile defense was achievable. Such a system, however, might take as much as twenty years and $250 billion to develop, although optimism was expressed over major technological breakthroughs in the early- and mid-1980s. The panel's overall findings offered enthusiastic support for continued research.

This prompted Dr. George Keyworth, the president's former science advisor, to comment: "This group of specialists, which included some of the most qualified defense scientists in the country, concluded that the president's goal was realistic—that it probably could be done." Dr. Keyworth referred to some of the key technical breakthroughs in computers and new laser techniques. He also mentioned the promising new developments that might enable us to protect the vitally important satellites carrying lasers and computers.

"These and other recent technical advances offer the possibility of a workable strategic missile defense system," he concluded.[3]

F O U R

THE REMARKABLE LASER

The real key to a successful SDI is a system that can knock down most, if not all, enemy missiles in their launch phase—before they have a chance to spread their multiple warheads. If such a system can destroy up to 80 percent or more of the enemy's missiles before they escape the earth's atmosphere, the major threat of a nuclear attack is thwarted.

This is the most vital part of SDI and it involves the most complex and demanding technologies. The answer lies in that remarkable device called the laser.

Laser is an acronym for *L*ight *A*mplification by the *S*timulated *E*mission of *R*adiation. Operating somewhat like a flashlight, the laser is a beam of light so concentrated that it can be projected for very long distances with relatively little loss of energy. At low power, it can carry signals, like a telephone wire. At high power, it can cut through a steel plate or, more to the point, could knock satellites out of space and destroy ballistic missiles within seconds of their launchings.

Currently, scientists and engineers are working on two types of laser systems. One calls for the placement of the lasers aboard satellites in space. The other would have ground-based lasers that would be beamed off huge mirrors in orbit back down to earth targets.

Both systems would rely on the critical electronic "eyes" of surveillance satellites in space. It is envisioned that such satellites, permanently placed in geosynchronous orbits 23,000 miles (37,000 km) high, would continuously scan the Soviet Union (or any other area for that matter), on the alert for any sign of an enemy missile attack. Heat-sensitive instrumentation aboard the spacecraft would instantly detect any telltale flames from a pending missile launch. This information would be relayed to computers that would calculate the probable course of the missile so a laser or other weapon could zero in on the target before it ever left its launchpad.

Theoretically, a fleet of laser-laden satellites could direct enough powerful beams of light to such targets hundreds or thousands of miles away and quickly destroy most, if not all, of the enemy's first-strike nuclear power.

Laser defensive weapons would work not by vaporizing their targets, as depicted in some science fiction movies, but by heating the skin of the target, or burning a hole in it. This would weaken the structure until it fractured or blew apart.

But the real key to a laser system is not its destructive power as much as its speed. Since light travels at a speed of about 186,000 miles (297,600 km) per second, a lethal blow could hit any target, even hundreds of thousands of miles away, almost instantaneously. For an example of what this means, consider that a laser light travels 1 mile (1.6 km) in six millionths of a second. In that same amount of time, a supersonic airplane, traveling at twice the speed of sound, will move only about one eighth of an inch.

Many experts now believe that the use of lasers will radically change warfare. Says Lieutenant General Kelly Burke, former air force chief of Research and Development: "It would equal the invention of gunpowder or of atomic explosives."

One drawback to a laser beam, being a beam of light,

is that it can be blocked by clouds and haze. For this reason, laser guns would work best in the pristine environment of space, far above the distortions of the earth's atmosphere. Also, from an orbital vantage point, lasers would have a direct line of sight to Soviet missiles.

Setting up laser defensive battle stations in space, however, will require enormous expense and the overcoming of a number of significant technological hurdles. In fact, only a few years ago many scientific experts called the whole idea of using lasers in space to shoot down ballistic missiles "pie in the sky."

One distinguished group, the Union of Concerned Scientists, flatly stated that an effective defense of the United States against Soviet missiles was "unattainable." A report prepared for the Office of Technology Assessment of the Congress called the chance of protecting the American people from a Soviet missile attack "so remote that it should not serve as the basis for public expectations or national policy."[4]

The critics' charges ranged over a broad spectrum. They said such a defense system in space would require thousands of satellites, each more expensive than an aircraft carrier. Reports said the power needed for spaceborne lasers would be equal to more than half the total power output of the United States. Critics further asked that even if a laser system in space could be developed, what would keep the Russians from developing a similar system of their own? This could lead to yet another expensive arms race costing countless billions of dollars. And, if both countries deploy such systems, they will simply cancel each other out, resulting in yet another standoff, like the one we are experiencing today with the nuclear arms race.

Despite these impressive arguments, the Reagan administration and the Department of Defense considered high-energy weapons such as the laser to be so important to the nation's future security that several billion dollars had already been spent by the mid-1980s on research, development, and testing.

One result of this intensive effort is the possibility of having the laser weapons based on earth rather than in orbit. Under this concept, free electron lasers would bounce high energy beams off orbiting space mirrors back down to enemy missiles. Lieutenant General James Abrahamson, head of the Strategic Defense Initiative, calls this one of the most promising futuristic weapons systems now on the drawing boards.[5]

The research work is being done at the Lawrence Livermore National Laboratory in California. There, prototype lasers combine breakthroughs in several technical fields to produce a beam that can be "tuned" to effectively penetrate the atmosphere and travel to targets halfway around the world.

U.S. Senator Malcolm Wallop of Wyoming, a strong advocate of laser weapons, said: "The lasers will not spell the end of war, but they at least hold the promise of barring nuclear-tipped missiles of mass destruction from the arena of war. These systems are purely defensive in nature. They cannot be used to harm human beings—only to destroy engines of mass destruction." (Because of the way they work, lasers would have no significant effect if they accidentally struck other targets, such as buildings.) "To be sure, the superpower that grasps the promise first will have an enormous strategic advantage."[6]

How will such systems work? The key components of a high-energy laser weapon include both the laser itself, which generates the light, and the beam-control subsystem, which aims the laser beam at the target and focuses it on a vulnerable spot. As with other weapons, the laser must also have a fire-control subsystem, which locates all the targets that need to be engaged, selects the one to engage first, then "tells" the beam-control subsystem where to look for it. Finally, the fire-control subsystem decides when the target has been destroyed and then designates the next target.

The Department of Defense (DOD) says that a single laser weapon can be expected to handle a large number of targets even if those targets, such as ballistic missiles, are coming from all directions at once. A 1980 DOD report estimated that twenty-five orbiting lasers could "kill" as many as one thousand ballistic missiles.

For each "shot" the laser takes, relatively small amounts of fuel are needed to generate the beam. Thus, there is the potential for storing a large number of "shots" per installation, either on the ground or in a satellite patrolling in space. Since the beam of light is steered by using mirrors, the laser weapon has the potential to move rapidly from target to target over a wide field of view.

There are, however, a number of major technical problems that must still be solved before a laser weapon system can become effective. For example, a successful laser attack would occur only when the beam burns through the target surface and destroys a vital component, such as the guidance system of a missile, or ignites a fuel tank or a nuclear warhead. So, although the energy is delivered instantaneously, the laser must dwell on the target long enough to destroy it.

Experts say that to damage its target effectively, a laser must focus on the subject for up to ten seconds. When the target is hundreds of miles away and moving, this requires an extremely precise system of aiming. For instance, if the beam of light "jitters," the energy is somewhat dispersed. This would increase the time required to damage the target. Therefore, the beam-control subsystem must hold the beam steady on the specific point aimed at. The situation may be further complicated by the distorting effects of the earth's atmosphere. To hold the beam steady, the target-tracking and beam-

On September 6, 1985, a laser lethality test was conducted at the White Sands Missile Range in New Mexico. The test target was the second stage of a Titan I booster missile body which contained no liquid propellant or explosives (top). In the test, the Titan was irradiated with a high-energy laser beam for several seconds before being destroyed (bottom). The laser used was the large chemical laser MIRACL (Mid-Infrared Advanced Chemical Laser), the most powerful continuous wave laser outside of the Soviet Union.

pointing functions of the beam-control subsystem must be extremely accurate.

The firing system for laser weapons must also be especially capable. It must be able to recognize and classify a host of potential targets, eliminating decoys and determining which target to strike first. Additionally, the fire control must be quick to recognize when the target has been damaged sufficiently, allowing the laser beam to move quickly then to the next target.

As mentioned earlier, the distorting effects of the atmosphere can cause a laser bean to "jitter" when directed toward a target on earth, increasing the time the beam needs to dwell on the target. In addition, bad weather or the presence of clouds or aerosols such as smoke can cause some of the energy in the laser beam to be absorbed, effectively limiting the range of the laser weapon. The dense air of the earth's atmosphere will disperse a laser beam and thus weaken it, especially over long distances, just as fog scatters the light from a car's headlamps. These are additional engineering problems that must be solved for lasers to work effectively as protective weapons.

Still another engineering problem is designing a laser system small and compact enough to be carried inside aircraft and satellites. Critics point out that by the time an effective laser weapons system can be developed, the enemy will have perfected countermeasures. These could include, for example, reflecting and rotating metal film parasols, mounted on targeted satellites, which could prevent laser destruction or the disabling of these satellites. Satellites could also be programmed to move around in orbit, evading attackers. Ground-based ballistic missiles could be protected with decoys, virtually impossible to distinguish from actual attacking missiles. Other possibilities include electronic jamming methods aimed at confusing lasers; enemy attacks on laser-armed satellites; and hardening missiles to withstand laser beams.

The cost of developing and placing a fully operational laser weapons system in space and/or on earth is staggering. Estimates have ranged from a low of $25 billion to a high of $1 trillion. The Defense Advanced Research Projects Agency (DARPA) has estimated the total cost of the initial laser battle station at $2.2 billion, but most experts feel the actual range of setting an entire system in place will be somewhere between $25 and $100 billion. Critics feel such costs are far too high for our economy to withstand, and that, with the feasibility of the weapons still in some doubt, they pose too great a financial risk.

But proponents of the laser system point out that these weapons could be used both offensively and defensively. As a defensive force, for example, they could be used against enemy killer satellites or other unfriendly systems. In this role, the defending satellite would have to establish a protective perimeter. If a hostile vehicle entered that perimeter, the attack would be launched. Some estimates suggest that a single laser station in space could attack as many as sixty satellites in one day.

The Department of Defense readily admits that a number of major obstacles must be overcome before the laser can become an effective weapons system, but military experts firmly believe that the necessary technological breakthroughs will be made and that a laser weapons system can become functional sometime between now and the end of this century. The exact time depends on how much emphasis is given to the development program.

DOD has already conducted a number of tests on a laser weapons system, with varying degrees of success. The first successful test occurred in 1973 when the air force used a high-energy gas laser of moderate power and a special telescope to shoot down a winged drone vehicle over the New Mexico desert.

Three years later, the army, using a high-energy electronic laser of relatively low power, destroyed winged and helicopter drones at its Redstone Arsenal in Alabama. In 1978, the navy, using a chemical laser of moderate power, successfully engaged and destroyed a TOW antitank missile at a site near San Juan Capistrano, California. This test series made believers out of many who had doubts about the future of the system.

The Defense Department explained that the major objectives of these experiments were to obtain experience and insight into the problems of integrating a laser of high power with a pointing and tracking device and maintaining the laser beam on the selected aimpoint, or target. The actual shootdowns, the Department said, while providing dramatic proof of attaining the technological goals, were actually a secondary objective.

In June 1981 the air force began experiments with a new airborne laser system, using a highly instrumented NKC-135 aircraft. Although results of these tests are classified, it was reported that the system failed twice to destroy air-to-air missiles. Still, scientists considered this only a temporary setback.

DARPA is deeply involved with several of the nation's leading aerospace contractor companies in a series of developmental programs generally known as the "Triad." The collective goal of these programs is to plan and eventually build a fully operational space-based battle station for the launching of lasers. Included within this series of programs are the following:

- Alpha—a program to manufacture a high-power hydrogen-flouride chemical laser.
- LODE (*L*arge *O*ptics *D*emonstration *E*xperiment)—a program to manufacture the optical system that will strengthen and extend the reach of the laser beam and send it on its way to the target.
- Talon Gold—a program to manufacture the pointing-tracking system that will spot a target, a

missile, or a satellite and track it, allowing the laser to fire accurately.

- SITT (System Integration of Triad Technology)—a program designed to integrate these three independent systems into a workable battle station.
- Teal Ruby—a program involving development of a sensor system that will initially allow the battle station to sense the heat exhaust of a missile in its launch phase, or even an enemy satellite in orbit with its radios turned off to keep it hidden in space.

"The American aerospace industry already is building chemical laser devices capable of generating up to ten million watts of light in space," says Senator Wallop. "It is also building mirrors capable of projecting that light thousands of miles away in doses powerful enough to destroy any known ballistic missile."

Meanwhile, U.S. intelligence sources report that the Russians are also working to develop high-power directed-energy weapons systems. It is known, for example, that the Soviets have conducted laser experiments aboard an orbiting laboratory in space.

It appears likely that at some point in the near future the United States will have to make a decision as to whether or not to go all-out in the development of laser weapons. President Ronald Reagan has already announced that the United States will develop a space-based ballistic missile defense. Many military experts say the most effective and lasting defense would employ laser systems.

According to current projections, laser-equipped satellites in space, or spatial battle stations, would orbit the earth at an altitude of roughly 800 miles (1,280 km). Each weapons system would have an effective range of some 3,000 miles (4,800 km). Each satellite would cover about 10 percent of the earth's surface, or about 20 million square miles (52 mllion sq km). Two dozen such satellites would have to be orbiting to cover every spot on the globe at any given time.

Each station would have enough fuel for about a thousand "shots." This means that each satellite would have enough laser ammunition, at least theoretically, to destroy up to one thousand enemy missiles, or other targets such as killer satellites, in an almost simultaneous barrage of fire.

As developments continue, more and more military experts are swinging toward the opinion that the key to future warfare, and especially war in space, will be space-based laser artillery focusing on the earth below and poised with beams of heat and light to destroy airplanes, missiles, satellites, or any other object. In such a setting, unmanned sentinel satellites, or manned spacecraft battle stations, could patrol the skies, armed with deadly cannons of light ready to smash any enemy vehicle on earth or in space. These weapons could be so awesomely accurate and powerful that a tank or battleship could not move on earth, or a satellite in orbit, without risking instantaneous attack and destruction by a deadly light beam unleashed from high above.

Although such a scene may paint a frightening picture of the future, there is a bright side to it, as expressed by Senator Wallop: "Technology is offering both to ourselves and the Soviet Union the opportunity to begin to overcome the vulnerable condition in which we have lived over the past decade . . . [and] the chance to move from purely offensive weapons and a strategy based on mass destruction to defensive weapons. I think this is an entirely happy prospect, so long as we are the ones who own the lasers."

F I V E

EXOTIC WEAPONRY

Another potential space weapon of the future is the particle beam. Essentially, this is an electron accelerator similar to those used by high-energy physicists to explore the inner properties of the atom.

A particle beam resembles a laser only to the extent that each weapon consists of a beam and is able to transfer its energy to the target at breathtakingly rapid speeds. The particle beam transmits thermal energy in much the fashion of a lightning bolt. Its effect on targets differs from lasers. Whereas lasers are designed to heat the surface of a target and weaken its structure, a particle beam eats through the skin and destroys the internal mechanisms. Since the laser consists of light, a cloudy day or a reflective coating on the target potentially could substantially reduce the laser's effectiveness. The weather does not hinder the performance of the ground-based particle beam, however.

DARPA says that particle beams, capable of delivering large amounts of energy at velocities near the speed of light and depositing them deep within a target, offer a wide range of potential applications for the military. For example, against nonnuclear threats such systems could provide a defensive shield ahead of advancing naval forces and defense of hardened missile sites against nuclear attack. In space, they could be used to strike earth targets where lasers might be ineffective because of weather conditions.[7]

Some scientists say particle beams would be the ultimate space-shield weapons because they travel at or near the speed of light and, in the vacuum of space, with unerring precision. Over the relatively short distances, several hundred or a few thousand miles, these beams would travel almost instantaneously, nearly eliminating the need to lead a target.

A space-borne battle station equipped with beam weapons could fire on the target, learn the results, and fire again repeatedly in less than a second, allowing one station to attack hundreds of targets within a few minutes. Because of their speed and accuracy, particle beams would do to the ballistic missile virtually what the machine gun did to the infantry charge.

However, particle-beam weapons will be even more difficult to develop than laser weapons. Because particle beams are charged particles, they are affected by the earth's magnetic field and demonstrate a disturbing tendency to bend once they leave the mouth of the accelerator that projects them. For this reason, and because of the extraordinary size of the generating system needed to produce a particle beam, many scientists agree that such a system is still much further in the future than a laser system and will probably cost even more to develop.

The Soviet Union, in talks with the United States, has indicated that it views particle-beam systems as weapons of mass destruction. The Russians claim, therefore, that according to the provisions of the Space Treaty, they cannot be used in space.

Still, leading U.S. aerospace technical journals have reported that the Soviet scientists are themselves "working seriously" on development of both laser and particle-beam weapons systems. *Aviation Week* and *Space Technology* magazines, for instance, have both cited "intense Soviet research on particle beams"; this has aroused fear

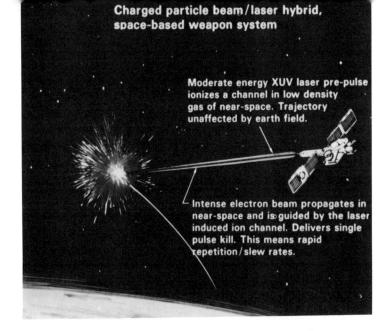

*A charged-particle beam/laser hybrid,
space-based weapon system*

in Congress and in some U.S. defense circles that the Russians are well on their way to a foolproof defense against missiles.

In the United States, theoretical and experimental research programs aimed at demonstrating the feasibility of creating charged particle beams in the atmosphere have been under way for more than twenty years. But these efforts have been limited because no means were available to provide the high-energy current and pulse repetition rates required. However, officials at DARPA say that a new accelerator now under development at the Lawrence Livermore National Laboratory may soon be able to demonstrate its ability to create particle beams within the atmosphere. Known as tne Advanced Test Accelerator, this elaborate device is designed to furnish information that will help the military plan experimental devices that could someday serve as the forerunners of future particle-beam weapons systems. Backers of the program say that if the difficult technological problems involved with the system can be overcome, the future deployment of both it and laser weapons systems could give the United States an impenetrable one-two defensive punch that would deter forever the threat of an enemy nuclear strike on the ground or in space.[8]

Beyond the development of "basic" laser weapons and particle beams, further out in the technology timetable, are some highly exotic systems which, if perfected, will offer even greater defense insurance against enemy missile attacks.

One such creation, for example, is the excimer laser. To make this work, an electron bombardment is used to ionize a gas such as xenon, which reacts with fluorine to form a gas that can be made to emit highly intense laser beams. These beams are so intense, in fact, they have the potential of breaking up a missile on impact.

Even more destructive, and more controversial, is the possibility of building X-ray lasers. While details of this program have been tightly wrapped in secrecy, it is known that the first step in the process is to explode a nuclear bomb. The laser would be mounted next to the nuclear weapon. When the bomb detonates, the laser is detroyed almost instantly, but in the fraction of a second before it is, the laser produces many beams of very intense X-rays that can be directed against enemy missiles and warheads with deadly effect.

Press reports have stated that scientists at the Lawrence Livermore Laboratory in California have successfully conducted an undeground test of an X-ray laser. The potential destructive power of this weapon is so awesome that some experts believe one X-ray laser no larger than a packing crate will be able to destroy the entire Russian ICBM arsenal, thousands of missiles, if they are launched at one time in a massive attack. '

Such dramatic weapons systems, however, will take longer to develop, possibly into the twenty-first century. But as the technical barriers continue to fall in laboratories across the nation, scientists may shorten that time span considerably.

S I X

"SMART BULLETS"

As scientists continue to work on a laser system, they realize that this "layer," the launch phase of a defensive shield, will take the longest to develop. Even with a number of major technological breakthroughs in recent years, it still will likely be the late 1990s or perhaps early into the twenty-first century before lasers can be effectively deployed, in space or on the ground, to give the United States the capability to knock out most of an enemy's intercontinental ballistic missile strike force.

This is not the case with other layers in the shield. Generally, two such layers are being considered. One has been called the "mid-course defense," or the "boost-phase defense." It is aimed at attacking missiles that escape the laser beams and accelerate through the earth's atmosphere enroute to their targets. The final layer has been called the "reentry" or "terminal" phase, and it is being designed to zero in on the nuclear warheads that have not been destroyed either at launch or during the mid-course of their flights.

The basic technology for both these layers already exists. No technical miracles are needed. Experts, in fact, believe this part of the Strategic Defense Initiative could be in place, protecting the United States, by the early 1990s.[9]

- 37

The mid-course defensive system would necessarily be based in space because it will depend on satellites for the surveillance of Soviet missile launching sites and the tracking of the missiles during their flight paths. The satellites also are needed to store the weapons designed to shoot down missiles.

The mid-course defense is more important than the reentry one for two reasons. First, it would have the capability to hit an enemy projectile before it had a chance to release its multiple warheads. Suppose a Soviet rocket is carrying ten separate nuclear warheads, each aimed at a specific target. Once these warheads have been released, the United States would have ten different objects to cover. But if the vehicle can be shot down before the warheads are sped on their way, ten targets are in effect killed with one blow.

Secondly, this layer of defense would mean the Russians would not know how to concentrate their warheads on U.S. targets because they would not know which missiles will get through such a defensive shield and which ones wouldn't. This would greatly complicate the strategy behind a nuclear first-strike launch. In other words, if the Russians were not sure what retaliatory targets would be knocked out, they would fear launching such an attack because the United States could respond with a nuclear strike of its own.

The key to this line of defense is called the "smart bullet." This is a projectile, much like today's air-to-air missile, that "homes in" on its target, using radar or heat waves, and destroys it on impact. Such missiles likely will be advanced versions of air defense interceptors that the U.S. Air Force uses today. They would be nonnuclear and would travel at a speed of 4 miles (6.4 km) per second.

Here's how they would work. Surveillance satellites in geosynchronous orbit 22,300 miles (35,680 km) above earth hover over the Russian missile launch sites. They would continuously scan for the telltale flames of a missile launch. Their sensitive instrumentation then would follow the course of the "bird" as it rises and pass the information along to computers that would calculate the probable flight path of the missile.

Literally within seconds, the computers could provide a picture of the entire attack, describing how many missiles are involved, which way they are going, and at what targets they are aimed. Once more, this data would be relayed—from the high-orbiting surveillance satellites to other satellites at lower altitudes, not far above the earth's atmosphere. These are the spacecraft carrying the smart bullets. Once they have locked onto their targets, their weapons fire.

The smart bullet senses its quarry either by radar reflections or by its delicate release of heat waves. Its computer brain then locks onto the flight path and directs projected flight-path messages to a cluster of rockets. Precise thrusts of these rockets steer it into the course of the missile or to individual warheads. The result is either destruction on impact or an explosion of the smart bullet when it hits the target. This releases a cloud of metallic fragments which will puncture the warhead, disabling its intricate electronics systems and thus disarming it. This has been likened to tossing a keg of nails into the flight path of the rocket or its warheads.

Actually, the smart bullet itself does not have to blow up the warhead. It only has to keep the nuclear weapon inside the warhead from exploding. This is not difficult since nuclear weapons do not easily explode.

Smart bullets are feasible because of the many technological advances that have been made in the miniaturization of computer circuits. These have enabled millions of transistors and other electronic components to be packed into a space the size of a thumbnail. Such devices are used to steer the weapon in flight with virtually unerring accuracy.

The final layer of the SDI shield, the so-called terminal phase, also will consist of smart bullets. This will be deployed in the near-earth atmosphere and is designed to destroy those missiles that seep through the first two layers of defense. These smart bullets will be ground based.

The goal here is to knock out these remaining missiles at altitudes of 50,000 feet (15,240 m) or higher so as to protect the ground from the possible impact of a nuclear explosion. At that height the effects, either in radioactive fallout or in blast effect, will not be too damaging.

These weapons will work similarly to those used in space. Rockets will launch the smart bullets to within a few miles of the rapidly moving warheads. Once in close proximity to the target, the bullets' instruments and computers will take over and maneuver them into a collision course for the kill.

Some experts believe this terminal portion of the shield can be developed and placed for $15 billion, including up to five thousand interceptors, plus aircraft that will carry instruments for acquisition and tracking of the warheads.

In recent years, tests of smart bullets have proven they can work, even though the distances, numbers, and velocities of intercontinental ballistic missiles will represent tougher targets than initial air-to-air and ground-to-air missiles were designed for. Upgrading these missiles to hit ICBMs, experts say, will merely call for some engineering fine-tuning.

In June 1984, for example, the U.S. Army fired a mock Soviet missile into space and then launched a smart bullet after it. The vehicle zeroed in on its target at 4,000 miles (6,400 km) per hour and destroyed it.

In September 1986, a Delta rocket was launched at Cape Canaveral, Florida, and orbited two satellites on a secret mission. An air force spokesman said the two pay-

An artist's concept of the U.S. Army's Homing Overlay Experiment (HOE) in which a homing-and-kill vehicle intercepts a mock Soviet missile above the mid-Pacific in June, 1984. Above the earth's atmosphere, an approximately 15-foot (4.5-m) diameter radial "net," wrapped tightly behind the nose sensor, unfurled like the ribs of an umbrella to increase the lethal radius of the homing-and-kill vehicle. The HOE vehicle and target closed at more than 15,000 feet (5,000 m) per second, smashed into each other, and shattered into tiny fragments.

loads used a variety of sensors to conduct observations during maneuvers from a variety of viewpoints. According to press reports, the payloads tracked each other in orbit for about four hours, then pointed at each other so that data on close-in approach could be obtained. The air force said the satellites then zeroed in on each other and both were destroyed.

The spokesman said the collision was a key test of kinetic energy technology, in which one projectile is hurled at another at great speed, demolishing the target. It was futher reported that objectives of the test were for the satellites to obtain spectral data on each other with infrared sensors and to test guidance, navigation, and thruster systems used in the maneuvering.

Lieutenant General James A. Abrahamson, head of SDI, called the test an unqualified success. He said another main objective of the test was fulfilled through the launch of an Aries rocket from the White Sands Missile Range in New Mexico. The satellites also tracked this rocket's rise to space before they collided.

Abrahamson said the idea here was to obtain data on what rocket plumes look like in space beyond the earth's atmosphere. Such information is essential for the development of sensors and guidance systems for smart bullets. Without the pressure of the earth's atmosphere to keep a rocket plume streaming in a straight line from the bottom of a missile, the plume expands and even envelopes a missile flying through space, the general said. It thus becomes critical to develop sensors that can guide a rocket to a missile body without being confused by the ball of hot exhaust gases.

Abrahamson also disclosed that the second stage of the Delta carried what he called "the world's first space-based laser radar." The device was described as low-powered, incapable of being used as a weapon, but as providing extremely accurate range data. The laser was used to point and steer the sensors on the second stage of the Delta rocket.

Also, many of the sensors employed during this $150 million experiment were derivatives of existing guidance systems. The second stage carried an infrared TV tracking system from the Maverick air-to-ground missile, while the third stage carried the radar guidance system used aboard the Phoenix air-to-air missile.

As practical, smart, and available technologically as these bullets are, they do have limitations. The problem is they would be fired toward their targets by rockets, which would serve as the "gun." Rockets would only get the smart bullet up to a speed of about 10,000 miles (16,000 km) per hour, which is about the same speed as the Soviet missile it would chase. This makes it difficult for the bullet to intercept the missile. It would have to be aimed in the missile's path, and considerably ahead of it, leading it, so to speak. The bullet's "brain," or computer, would have to anticipate where the missile is going to be several minutes and several thousand miles from where it is at the point when the bullet is fired. This is a difficult task. Plus, a smart bullet has a limited capacity for maneuvering, and if the prediction of the missile's position is not accurate enough to bring the bullet close to the target, the bullet's computer will not be able to steer it into a collision.

To compensate for this in the future, scientists are working on a new system of bullet projection called the electromagnetic railgun. It would not itself destroy a missile, but used in combination with smart bullets, it could greatly enhance their effectiveness. It would do this by flinging the smart bullets spaceward at much greater speeds than are attainable today.

It would work something like this: The bullet would be mounted on a sliding carriage between two rails. An electric current of several million amperes would flow down one rail and up the other, creating an extremely intense magnetic field between the rails. This magnetic field would propel the bullet forward. Dr. Robert Jastrow has said such a gun eventually may be able to propel bul-

In September, 1986, at White Sands Missile Range, a Patriot missile is fired to intercept a Lance missile which had been fired as a target. Upon the Patriot missile hitting its target (inset), the damaged Lance missile, trailing smoke, is starting to fall to earth, out of control after the intercept, while the fireball is from the Patriot missile.

*An artist's concept of a space-
based electromagnetic railgun firing
"smart bullets" at enemy missiles*

lets at speeds greater than 50,000 miles (80,500 km) per
hour, or five times the speed of an incoming enemy missile. At such a pace, a smart bullet could intercept a missile a thousand miles away in less than a minute.

But like the laser and the particle beam, the railgun
needs more advanced technologies before it can become
a reality. Some experts believe it could be developed
sometime in the mid to late 1990s.

– 45

S E V E N

IMPASSE IN ICELAND

Any doubt that the Soviets greatly fear America's Strategic Defense Initiative was dramatically dispelled at a superpower summit meeting of U.S. and Soviet leaders held at Reykjavik, Iceland, on October 11 and 12, 1986. There, President Ronald Reagan and Soviet leader Mikhail Gorbachev met for eleven hours of intensive talks aimed at finding a way to reduce nuclear arms.

For a while, it appeared that a revolutionary agreement might be reached. This would have included banning all medium range nuclear missiles from Europe and working toward a phaseout of all nuclear testing. But the headline proposal was to reduce all strategic nuclear missile strike forces within five years and to eliminate them completely within ten years. This was perhaps the most promising and comprehensive proposal to reduce nuclear arms since the atom bomb became a reality in the 1940s.

But toward the end of the second day of talks, Gorbachev demanded that such an agreement could only be reached if the United States would, in effect, scrap its plans for building a defense system in space. Specifically, he asked that research on SDI be limited to laboratory work for the next ten years. He also contended that SDI was not a defensive, but a first-strike offensive weapons system. Gorbachev asserted that SDI actually was part of an American effort to build a first-strike nuclear force that could leave the United States invulnerable to Soviet retaliation.

The Soviets, in fact, have long feared SDI, and have expressed their concern about it ever since Reagan first announced the concept in his 1983 speech. Marshal Sergei Akhromeyev, chief of the Soviet general staff, has said, for example, that the Russian concern is not the creation of an effective defensive shield, but the "spillover" from SDI research and development, which he expects would create technological breakthroughs in both strategic and conventional weaponry in the years ahead.

The Soviets also insist that space-based American weapons, which Reagan sees as defensive, would pose a serious offensive threat to Russia. They argue that laser weapons in space would be more effective as part of a carefully timed offensive attack than in a scramble to defend against a surprise Soviet strike.

The Soviets say SDI would be particularly dangerous for them if the two countries engaged in the kind of massive reductions of offensive weapons they were discussing in Iceland. The Soviet Union now has a small but real advantage in offensive, land-based missiles. If they volunteer to relinquish it through reductions while the United States went ahead with strategic defense, they argue, they would soon find themselves at a disadvantage.

Gorbachev summed up this point when he said at a postsummit news conference: "We understand now that the U.S. administration is out to make a breakthrough with SDI to military superiority."

When Gorbachev brought up these points in Iceland, Reagan countered, hoping to allay Soviet fears, by offering to delay deployment of any part of SDI for ten years, while research and development work continued. Gorbachev turned this proposal down, and the nuclear arms reduction talks collapsed.

At a postsummit press conference, U.S. Secretary of State George Shultz said, "It has been clear for a long time, and it was certainly clear today, the importance the Soviet leader attaches to the Strategic Defense Initiative. . . . As we came more and more down to the final stages (of negotiation), it became more and more clear that the Soviet Union's objective was to effectively kill off the SDI program.

"The president simply would not turn away from the basic security interests of the United States, or allies and the free world, by abandoning this essential defensive program," Shultz said. "He had to bear in mind that not only is the existence of the strategic defense program a key reason why we were able potentially to reach these agreements [on missile reductions], but undoubtedly its continued existence and potential would be the kind of program you need in the picture to insure yourself that the agreements reached would be effectively carried out.

"And so in the end, with great reluctance, the president . . . simply had to refuse to compromise the security of the United States, of our allies and freedom, by abandoning the shield that has held in front of freedom."

When asked by a reporter if we had lost the chance to reduce nuclear weapons because of SDI, Shultz answered: "That is not the way we must think about it because, while we had set out many sweeping and potentially very significant things, if they only came to pass as a result of scuttling the SDI program, then you have to ask yourself if they would really have come to pass after all, after the SDI program was gone."

Shultz later said continued strong work on SDI would be required even after negotiated reduction of offensive arms began because "The promise of strategic defense is the thing that would help deliver future reductions." In other words, the threat that we could deploy an SDI system is now seen as the best guarantee that the Soviets will remain in compliance with any agreement to reduce offensive nuclear weapons.

On October 13, 1986, the day after the summit, President Reagan addressed the nation to explain why he did what he did.

I offered a proposal that we continue our present research [on SDI] and if and when we reached the stage of testing, we would sign now a treaty that would permit Soviet observation of such tests. And if the program was practical, we would both eliminate our offensive missiles, and then we would share the benefits of advanced defenses.

I explained that even though we would have done away with our offensive ballistic missiles, having the defense would protect against cheating or the possibility of a madman sometime deciding to create nuclear missiles. After all, the world now knows how to make them. I likened it to our keeping our gas masks even though the nations of the world had outlawed poison gas after World War I.

. . . the General Secretary [Gorbachev] wanted wording that in effect would have kept us from developing the SDI for the entire ten years. In effect, he was killing SDI and unless I agreed, all that work toward eliminating nuclear weapons would go down the drain—cancelled."

I told him [Gorbachev] I had pledged to the American people that I would not trade away SDI—there was no way I could tell our people their government would not protect them against nuclear destruction.

I realize some Americans may be asking tonight: "Why not accept Mr. Gorbachev's demand? Why not give up SDI for this agreement?" The answer, my friends, is simple. SDI is America's insurance policy that the Soviet

Union will keep the commitments made at Reykjavik. SDI is America's security guarantee if the Soviets should—as they have done too often in the past—fail to comply with their solemn commitments.

SDI is what brought the Soviets back to arms control talks in Geneva and Iceland. SDI is the key to a world without nuclear weapons.

E I G H T

THE NEW HIGH GROUND

The United States is pledged to preserving space for peaceful use and the benefit of all humanity. This objective is backed by international law and treaties with other nations restricting the exploitation of space, the moon, and other celestial bodies. Also, as decreed by treaties, weapons of mass destruction, such as nuclear bombs, are not to be tested or placed in orbit.

However, faced with the steady advances being made in space technology by the Soviet Union, the United States feels compelled not only to help uphold international law and its treaty obligations, but also to try to maintain its leading role in space technology, so as to ensure against unfriendly nations exploiting space for their own military purposes. This mission has been charged to the U.S. Air Force.

The National Aeronautics and Space Act of 1958, which created the National Aeronautics and Space Administration (NASA), also designated the Department of Defense (DOD) to be responsible for and to direct "those activities peculiar to or primarily associated with the development of weapons systems, military operations, or the defense of the United States, including the research and development necessary to make effective provisions for the defense of the United States."

Adding to this, Dr. Hans Mark, former secretary of the air force, in testimony before the U.S. House of Representatives Subcommittee on Space Science and Applications, said in April 1981:

Our charter of the Department of Defense is very broad and comprehensive. Today, twenty-two years after enactment of the 1958 Space Act, our activities in space are crucial to the security of the United States.

There are two missions above all others that stand out as being of vital importance to the national security. One has to do with providing timely warning of possible attacks by strategic missiles that the Soviet Union or other nations possessing them might launch. Our strategic deterrent forces depend heavily on warning, which will allow our strategic bombers on alert to get off in time, as well as for a number of other activities related to the readiness of our strategic forces. Satellites provide these warnings or signals. They give the alert that allows the bombers adequate time to taxi to the runways and take off.

The second function is surveillance. Surveillance is equally important because we depend heavily upon space systems to know what our potential adversaries around the world are doing. In the last few years, we have unfortunately lost routine access to large regions of the world, such as Afghanistan, Ethiopia, Iran, and Angola. Our space systems have accordingly become much more important.

The air force has long considered space an extension of its domain. Because there is no distinct boundary between air and space, the air force has seen its responsibility for defense as one without specific altitude limitations.

As early as 1959, General Thomas D. White, then

chief of staff of the U.S. Air Force, said: "The air force has operated throughout its relatively short history in the sensible atmosphere around the earth. Recent developments have allowed us to extend our operations farther away from the earth—approaching the environment referred to as space. Since there is no dividing line, no natural barrier separating these two areas, there can be no operational boundary between them. Thus, air and space comprise a single continuous operational field in which the air force must continue to function. This area is aerospace."

Twenty-one years later, General Alton D. Slay, then commander of Air Force Systems, added: "Space isn't a mission; it's a place, an environment; an arena of considerable operational mission import, but certainly not a 'mission,' per se, any more than the atmosphere or the ocean or the land is a mission. We have a mission 'in space,' not a 'space mission.' "

The development of U.S. space policy and current U.S. space operations is a natural outgrowth of the development of air power. The air force has found that some of its functions can be performed better in space than in the atmosphere or on earth. In essence, the air force operates in space because it makes military and economic sense to be there. The air force is there to provide support to the nation's terrestrial forces.

Basically, the air force is charged with three general missions in space. It organizes, trains, equips, and sustains forces to conduct operations for *space support, force enhancement*, and *space defense*.

Space support involves activities critical to the success of ongoing space missions. That is, the air force must provide sufficient space-technology development, launch support, monitoring, and logistics (supply and maintenance) support to conduct its long-term space operations.

One example of this is the work the air force has done

in cooperation with NASA on the space shuttle, which flies a large number of military missions. For instance, the air force is developing an inertial upper stage (IUS) for the shuttle that will enable the United States to boost satellites and other payloads into orbits higher than the shuttle flies.[10]

Force enhancement involves space operations that can greatly improve the responsiveness and readiness of the land, sea, and aerospace forces of the United States. This includes the orbiting and monitoring of satellites for improved communications, more precise navigational aids, better and more extensive weather information, more reliable and faster warning of attack, and improved surveillance.

Space defense includes operations that help defend the United States against attacks from or through space. This also involves the defense of all United States assets and interests in space.

As the value of space systems to the United States increases, so, too, does the need to protect them. Recent technological advances by foreign nations mean that space may no longer be considered the safe haven for the United States that it once was. Future systems must be deployed with protection and survival in mind.

This need is underscored, for example, by recent Soviet achievements in the antisatellite weapons field. Such systems jeopardize all American craft in space. The United States is responding to this threat in several ways. To prevent a new kind of arms race, such as an antisatellite arms race, the United States held talks with the Soviets aimed at suspending further antisatellite activity.

However, no agreements have yet come out of these talks. Therefore, the air force is moving to protect its space systems by improving its monitoring of space activities, reducing the vulnerability of United States satellites, developing an antisatellite capability against hostile spacecraft, and improving on the management of all space defense resources. Space will play a greater role in future air force operations, and as the military value of space increases, so will the importance of space defense.

To prepare for this, the air force has developed a Consolidated Space Operations Center (CSOC), which consists of two elements: a Satellite Operations Center and a Shuttle Operations and Planning Center. It combines in a single facility all the elements necessary to conduct both shuttle and satellite mission operations.

The satellite Operations Center handles communications functions, issues flight commands, and otherwise controls the orbital missions of military spacecraft. The Space Shuttle Operations and Planning Center conducts DOD shuttle flight planning and launch preparations. This center also has direct overall control of all DOD shuttle missions.

This space headquarters is staffed by about three hundred military personnel, one hundred air force civilians, and fourteen hundred civilian employees who are under contract to the air force.

N I N E

A PROUD HERITAGE

Although the space age was officially opened on October 4, 1957, with the successful launching of the tiny Soviet satellite *Sputnik* into earth orbit, the concept of using space for military purposes predates this by a number of years. Fifteen years and one day before *Sputnik* was orbited, on October 3, 1942, an event took place that, perhaps more than any other single occurrence, set the precedence for today's space-weapons race.

The place was a remote site called Peenemunde, on the northern German coast. There, a team of brilliant scientists and engineers, headed by space pioneer Wernher von Braun, successfully test-launched the first V-2 rocket. It weighed 14 tons and reached an altitude of only 50 miles (80 km). This was far short of earth oribt, but the Germans knew even then that it was only a matter of time and priorities before earth orbit would be achieved also.

The V-2 was the forerunner of today's mighty ICBMs. Although crude by today's standards, during the latter years of World War II the V-2 wreaked terror and destruction on England. Still, only a few people realized fully then what the V-2 would lead to. One who did was German general Walter Dornberger, who said to von

Braun: "Do you realize what we accomplished today? Today, the spaceship was born."

Von Braun also recognized the significance of that first successful launch. In March 1944, he said, "The V-2 was not intended as a weapon of war. I had space travel in mind when it was developed, and I regretted its imminent operational use."

Looking back, some experts have called the development of the V-2 rocket the greatest leap forward in technology that had been made up to that time. In fact, it has been compared in technological importance with the creation of the atomic bomb a short time later.

At the end of World War II, the German rocket team that built the V-2 was split up. Von Braun and many of his associates came to the United States to help it build a military missile program. Others went to the Soviet Union for the same purpose.

U.S. Air Force space activities accelerated in 1954 with the creation of the nation's first ballistic missile program. Out of this program came the ICBMs that today are a major portion of the nation's strategic deterrance force.

Ironically, the United States could have been the first nation in space, beating *Sputnik*, if military rockets had been used. By the mid-1950s, the von Braun team had developed powerful Redstone and Jupiter missiles capable of projecting small satellites into earth orbit. Von Braun pleaded with government officials to use these vehicles for just such a purpose.

But U.S. president Dwight D. Eisenhower turned the request down because the Redstone was a military rocket, and he wanted to emphasize the peaceful uses of space. Eisenhower instead ordered development of a completely new rocket system, the Vanguard. But before it could get off the ground, the Soviets launched *Sputnik I* and followed a month later with the flight of *Sputnik II*, which carried a dog into orbit. These accomplishments shocked both the United States and the rest of the free world and gave the Soviet Union a tremendous technological and propaganda victory over the United States. To compound U.S. frustrations, the first U.S. satellite launch attempt with the Vanguard, on December 6, 1957, ended in embarrassing failure when the rocket exploded on its launchpad during takeoff.

At that time von Braun again asked the U.S. Defense Department to let his team try. "Vanguard will never make it," he said. "We have the hardware on the shelf. For God's sake, turn us loose and let us do something. We can put up a satellite in sixty days."

Finally given the okay, the von Braun team successfully orbited America's first satellite, *Explorer I*, on January 31, 1958, beginning a space race that was to reach a climax in July 1969, with the United States landing the first humans on the moon.

In October 1958, the National Aeronautics and Space Act, creating the United States civilian space agency NASA, was enacted. The air force also derives its present space mission from this act. It is the legal basis for all U.S. military and civilian space activities. NASA has responsibility for all U.S. civilian space programs; the air force is the branch of the military responsible for almost all U.S. defense activity in space.

The air force coordinates with NASA on projects of mutual interest. Within the air force, the Air Force Systems Command manages most military space operations. This includes space-related research and development, testing, and engineering and support in the launching, operation, and maintenance of military space systems.

For a number of years most of NASA's satellites and spacecraft were boosted into space by military rockets. For example, the Redstone rocket launched astronauts Alan B. Shepard, Jr., and Virgil I. ("Gus") Grissom in 1961 into suborbital flights, and an Atlas booster launched the historic first manned American orbital flight, of John Glenn, in February 1962, as well as other manned orbital flights in the Mercury and Gemini programs during the 1960s.

Overall, between 1958 and 1972, of the seven-hundred-plus payloads the United States placed in earth, solar, or lunar orbit, more than two-thirds of them were sent up by military rockets. Modified versions of air force's Atlas, Titan, and Thor rockets were used for years to launch a variety of NASA satellites for weather observation, communications, and scientific missions. The air force's Agena vehicle helped send the first spacecraft on long-distance flights past the planets Venus and Mars.

T E N

GLOBAL COMMUNICATIONS

In the past two decades, satellites have revolutionized the communications field. Today, nearly any event or activity taking place in the world can be relayed instantly via satellite to viewers thousands of miles away. Such capabilities offer many advantages to the military.

Actually, the concept of using orbiting satellites to relay communications originated in 1945 with the famous science fiction writer Arthur C. Clarke, who described such satellites as microwave relay stations in space. The launch of the Soviet Union's *Sputnik* twelve years later spurred U.S. military and commercial efforts to develop Clarke's idea, now that placing satellites in orbit was shown to be feasible. In the next few years, a number of experimental communications satellites were launched into space, including *Score*, *Echo*, *Courier*, *Telstar*, *Syncom*, *Relay*, *Early Bird*, and *Intelsat*. The success of these civilian satellites led the military to the development of its own satellite systems.

For communications purposes, satellites offer unique advantages because they overcome the "ground-based" problems involved in spanning oceans and continents for the long-distance transmission of radio, telephone, and television signals. Because microwaves travel only in a straight line, for example, relay stations on earth must be placed every 35 miles (56 km) or so, to allow for the transmitting of signals around the curve of the earth. To set up this many stations around the world would be prohibitively expensive. Similarly, submarine cables cost a lot to install and maintain and generally have limited capability.

One satellite, however, placed in orbit approximately 22,300 miles (35,680 km) above the earth at the equator, can remain over one spot on earth and provide communications relay coverage across an ocean or two or more continents. Three satellites spaced at 120-degree intervals can effectively cover the entire earth. The satellites remain in place because at this altitude their speed in orbit matches the rotational speed of the earth. They appear to hover over one spot. Such an orbit is generally known as geosynchronous orbit.

Today, military satellites provides essential and immediate defense communications for worldwide command and control. Satellites can be designed to send messages to small mobile or portable users, thus allowing quick reaction to crises in remote areas. At the same time, they can be employed for high-volume communications traffic between any two points where large earth terminals can be situated. And, such systems can be developed to have a high degree of survivability against physical or electronic attack.

Military communications satellites fulfill strategic as well as tactical missions. Strategic missions tie satellites to a group of fixed earth stations; hence, communications can be established over any path on which two or more stations are mutually "visible" to orbiting spacecraft. The tactical system permits communications between satellites and a variety of earth stations that may include mobile ones such as those in aircraft, ships, automobiles, or even properly equipped soldiers in the field.

How effective are communications from space for military purposes? During the Vietnam War, satellites regularly transmitted high-speed digital data from South Vietnam to Defense Department headquarters at the Pentagon just outside Washington, D.C. Within minutes after processing, high-quality reconnaissance photographs of battle zones were available to Pentagon analysts, via the Defense Department's Initial Defense Satellite Communications System.

Currently, about two-thirds of U.S. long-distance military message traffic is routed through space. The bulk of this traffic, including up-to-the-minute intelligence data on such things as worldwide troop movements and deployment, is handled by the Defense Satellite Communications Systems (DSCS). DSCS was begun in 1966 and has evolved in three phases.

Phase one consisted of twenty-six small satellites launched between 1966 and 1968. These pioneering spacecraft had only one channel each and were designed to last three years, though one operated for more than ten years. This first phase provided highly efficient communications globally and paved the way for phase two.

This phase, still in service, consists of four active satellites and two spares. Each spacecraft has four channels and upon failure is replaced by a new satellite. These "second-generation" craft carry many times the communications loads of those used in phase one. The air force says that this capability supports vital national security requirements for worldwide command and control, crises management, intelligence data relay, diplomatic traffic, and early-warning detection and reporting of enemy-launched missiles.

The air force has also developed the Fleet Satellite Communications System (FLTSATCOM), which provides high priority, jam-resistant, near-global communications to the air force, navy, and other government users. The system has five satellites, each with twenty-

*A third-phase Defense Satellite
Communications System (DSCS), used to
collect up-to-the-minute intelligence data*

three communications channels. Ten are for navy use, twelve are for air force use as a part of its overall satellite communications network, and the one remaining channel is reserved for use by National Command Authorities, which includes the president, the secretary of defense, and the chairman of the Joint Chiefs of Staff. This system provides communication links among naval aircraft ships, submarines, and ground stations—and Strategic Air Command and National Command Authorities networks. Receiving terminals are installed in air force command post aircraft, strategic bombers, tanker aircraft, and in selected ground command centers. The army and navy also have terminals to receive communications data from these satellites.

The system additionally provides worldwide, direct, one-hundred-words-per-minute teletype communications to and from the National Command Authorities, military commanders, and those in charge of the U.S. nuclear forces. At present, the communications capabilities and positioning of air force communications satellites are centrally controlled from the Air Force Satellite Test Center in Sunnyvale, California, through a network of Satellite Control Facility stations.

In 1982, the air force launched the first of a test series of DSCS satellites—phase three. These advanced craft are designed for longer life, increased channelization, user flexibility, and greater antijam protection. The air force launched several of these DSCS-III satellites in the mid-1980s to replace the phase-two series and to provide continuous orbital communications capabilities through the mid-1990s.

E L E V E N

MILITARY METEOROLOGY

For years the Department of Defense has used earth-orbiting meteorological satellites for the collection and quick dissemination of weather information. Accurate weather forecasts have been a basic need of military commanders throughout history. This type of data is invaluable in wartime. Such conditions as fog, rain, sleet, snow, clouds, and wind are often instrumental in land, sea, and air military decisions. Often bad weather is seen as a disadvantage, holding up important launchings or attacks. At other times, adverse weather conditions are seen as advantageous, useful as a camouflaging screen to protect troop, ground vehicle, ship, or aircraft movements. Battle plans are drawn up only after all the meteorological data are studied and evaluated. Thus, the ability to survey and "weather map" the entire earth from space on a daily, hourly, or even minute-by-minute basis is of vital importance to military planning and operations even in peaceful times, because with such advanced weaponry as ICBMs and nuclear bombs, U.S. defense forces must today be constantly alert, ready to respond to any threat or enemy attack within moments.

Satellites laden with sensitive instruments and unblinking electronic "eyes" can scan the entire globe, continually relaying thousands of pictures of weather conditions as they develop to ground stations around the world. Such craft, from several hundred miles above the earth, tirelessly make passing sweeps of the entire planet in less than two hours, covering the North Pole, going south across the continents and oceans until they are over Antarctica, then heading north again. Pictures and data stored during these continuous passes are relayed from space to ground stations, where, through complex computer networks, the information is speedily analyzed, then flashed to receiving stations in the United States and elsewhere around the world. This enables military meteorologists today to make the fastest, most accurate weather forecasts ever.

The U.S. Air Force developed in the early 1970s a new system—the Defense Meteorological Satellite Program, or DMSP. By ringing the earth with a new series of instrumented satellites, up-to-the-minute weather information in every part of the world could be instantly relayed to ground, sea, and airborne stations.

"Weather data is very perishable with time," says John L. McLucas, former secretary of the air force. "The DMSP system has been designed to provide decision makers with weather data within minutes of its collection in space. The space segments of the system consist of infrared and visual sensors. The infrared sensors' products are images of the earth and its atmosphere that are representative of temperatures rather than brightness, while the visual sensors detect the brightness of reflected solar illuminations."

McLucas says that monitoring storms, including typhoons and hurricanes, on a global basis is one of DMSP's major applications and that data gathered by the system's satellites are made available to the public to gain maximum use of what he called "this national resource." Information gathered by DMSP satellites is sent to the Commerce Department's National Oceanic and Atmospheric Administration (NOAA), which may then pass that information to the civilian community.

How does the air force use these satellites today? By analyzing the data relayed from space, military weather forecasters detect and observe developing patterns and follow existing weather systems. The data helps the forecasters to identify severe weather conditions such as thunderstorms and determine the intensity of hurricanes and typhoons. In addition, it provides imagery to form three-dimensional cloud analysis of various weather conditions.

DMSP satellites are capable of providing weather data on a real-time (as it's happening) basis to the Air Weather Service and navy, or they can store the data for later transmission to Fairchild Air Force Base in Washington or Loring Air Force Base in Maine. Recorded data is also received at an air force station in Hawaii. All of these sites, as well as the Command Control Center at Offutt Air Force Base in Nebraska, are operated by the Strategic Air Command's Aerospace Applications Group. By use of communications satellites, the data received are relayed from both readout sites and the Hawaii tracking station to Air Force Global Weather Central at Offutt.

For any given geographic location, mobile ground terminals can provide military commanders in the field with photographiclike prints of cloud cover four times a day. The Mark IV mobile ground terminal is a compact unit consisting of a 10-foot (3-m) parabolic antenna, a van, and an auxiliary power generator. The entire transportable terminal is compact enough to be carried in a C-130 aircraft.

As DMSP satellites pass overhead, the mobile ground terminals receive pictures of a section of the earth and its cloud cover. Weather data transmitted from the satellites to the ground terminal can be gridded and

*DMSP (Defense Meteorological Satellite Program)
satellites provide real-time (as it's happening)
weather information in every part of the world,
for use by ground, sea, and airborne stations.*

labeled for clarification. The system's technology also
permits weather watchers to enlarge and print selected
portions of infrared and visual weather data from both
the DMSP and NOAA satellites.

Normally, there are two DMSP satellites in orbit at
any one time. They circle the earth at an altitude of about
390 miles (594 km) in a near-polar orbit and make one
complete revolution every 101 minutes. Each satellite
scans a 1,400-mile-wide (2,240-km) area, and each can
cover the entire earth in about twelve hours.

The satellites each weigh about three quarters of a
ton on earth, including 400 pounds (180 kg) of sensor

payload. When deployed in space, with their solar arrays extended, they are 4 feet (1.2 m) wide and 21 feet (6.3 m) long. Each satellite is divided into four major sections:

- a precision mounting platform for sensors and other equipment requiring precise alignment;
- an equipment support module that encloses the bulk of the sophisticated electronics;
- A reaction-control equipment support structure containing the spent third-stage rocket motor and the ascent-phase reaction-control equipment; and
- a solar-cell array.

The Operational Linescan System is the primary sensor onboard the satellites, providing visual and infrared imagery day or night. This data is used to analyze cloud patterns in support of a wide range of military requirements, from selecting aerial refueling stations to issuing severe weather condition warnings.

From different heights within the atmosphere, temperature/moisture sounders measure infrared radiation, allowing forecasters to plot temperature and water vapor by altitude. A microwave temperature sounder is also used, to measure the amount of microwave radiation present at different heights within the atmosphere. This allows forecasters to plot temperature versus altitude curves over even cloudy regions of the globe. A precipitating electron spectrometer is used to forecast the location and intensity of the aurora (the "northern lights") and to aid radar operations and long-range ground communications in the Northern Hemisphere. With all this sensitive and extremely accurate instrumentation in place, constantly orbiting the earth, the military can plan precise maneuvers and operations anywhere in the world, fully assured of what the exact weather conditions will be.

T W E L V E

A NEW ORDER OF NAVIGATION

The idea for a navigational satellite system can actually
be traced back more than a century. In his story "The
Brick Moon," published in 1869, Edward Everett Hale
envisioned a large artificial satellite circling the earth in
an orbit over the poles and passing along the Greenwich
Meridian. Hale reasoned that ships could take bearings
on this artificial "moon" and thus more accurately fix
their positions at sea.

Ninety years later, in 1959, the U.S. Navy launched
Transit 1A, the first real navigational satellite, to help
guide its submarines. Several more spacecraft were
orbited over the next several years, and by the early
1970s both the United States and the Soviet Union had
operational systems, used primarily for the benefit of
subs and a few of the larger surface ships.

Before these satellites were available for pinpointing
the location of fleet ballistic-missile submarines, the
navy frequently experienced navigational errors of 2 to 3
miles (3.2 to 4.8 km) in good weather, and as much as 50
miles (80 km) in bad weather. The first network of navigational satellites, however, made it possible to "fix"
one's position with errors as small as the length of a submarine or even smaller.

A successful orbital navigational system depends upon accurately knowing the satellite's position, then finding one's own position—be it in an aircraft or on a ship—relative to it. In other words, the satellite becomes a known landmark, the only one always visible on the broad oceans. Stars are used in the same manner in stellar navigation, but they are not always visible.

The advantage of a navigational satellite is that signals can be sent out, received by the satellite, and analyzed by computers all in a very short time. The information can then be transmitted back to the craft, giving the pilot his or her location rapidly and continuously. The satellites operate under all weather conditions and can supply position information to ships (or aircraft) anywhere.

The navy uses a number of satellites in circular, near-polar orbits about 600 miles (960 km) above the earth. Twice a day the orbits to be followed are calculated by tracking stations for each of the satellites, and these data are transmitted to the spacecraft's memory unit. Each satellite then supplies the appropriate orbital data at two-minute intervals.

Navigators on submarines or surface ships determine when the satellite is directly overhead by analyzing its radio signals, which change as the satellite approaches, then recedes from, the vessel. This information, together with the orbital data, the time the signal was received, and the speed of the ship, is fed into a computer aboard the ship, which rapidly calculates and fixes the ship's exact position.

The Transit navigational satellite system has been called the greatest advance in position-fixing in more than two hundred years. For example, even relatively inexpensive satellite-receiving sets today give ships at sea constantly updated latitude and longitude readings accurate within 200 yards (180 m). By comparison, mariners using the traditional sextant to determine their ships' positions (by "shooting" the sun or stars) consider an error of 2 miles (3.2 km) as generally acceptable.

Although the Transit system was developed by the navy for use in the precise positioning at all times of nuclear submarines and other military ships, it is also used extensively by civilian groups. Merchant ships worldwide, properly equipped with receiving equipment, can get up-to-the-minute information on their exact positions and courses at sea. Tuna boats ranging far into the ocean use navigational satellites not only to return to places where the fishing is good, but also to make printouts from their receivers to prove that they haven't sailed in restricted fishing zones. The satellite system has also been adapted for the charting of offshore oil and mineral deposits and for land-survey projects.

Commenting on what navigational satellites can mean to business, former U.S. Congressman Joseph Karth of Minnesota said: "The Maritime Administration and industry people in the shipping field have been looking to the day of the automated ship. This is a ship that will leave port in the United States with a crew consisting of a handful of people, primarily electronics specialists, who will operate and maintain the computers and other specialized equipment. The satellite-position information would be fed directly into a ship's computers. The ship would stay on a perfect prescribed course to its final destination. Of prime importance, too, is air traffic control and maritime coordination. Collision avoidance can be greatly improved by the use of such a combination of communications and navigation systems."

Through the years the navy has upgraded its spatial navigation systems and in 1981 launched the first of a new series of satellites, the NOVAs, an advanced version of Transit designed to meet the navy's navigation-by-space needs throughout the decade of the 1980s. These new vehicles will orbit at an altitude of about 600 miles (960 km) and provide worldwide weather navigational data for the navy and commercial ships. Improvements in NOVA include a stronger transmitter, increased computer memory, and an ability to compensate for orbital disturbances. The navy says that no changes to existing Transit-user equipment are necessary to use the newer NOVA system.

Another new space system—the air force's Navstar Global Positioning System—promises radically improved navigation. Through a network of satellites and receivers, this system will provide continuous worldwide positioning and navigational data. Navstar will consist of eighteen satellites placed in orbit about 11,000 miles (17,600 km) above the earth.

Each satellite will continually transmit its position and the precise time of transmission. Receiving sets on the ground, in aircraft, or on ships will receive signals from four different satellites, and this data will be processed by a sophisticated system that can compare the signals and thereby determine exact position and altitude. By analyzing this information, a military user will be able to tell his or her exact position as well as altitude anywhere on earth to within 50 feet (15 m).

How will such data be used by the military? Navstar will aid in weapons delivery to a precise target; enroute navigation for all military space, air, land, and sea vehicles; military aircraft runway approach; photo-mapping; geodetic surveys; aerial rendezvous for refueling; tactical missile navigational systems updating; air-traffic control; improved range instrumentation and safety; as well as more accurate search-and-rescue operations.

Very simple receivers will allow soldiers to plot their position and to aim their artillery with extreme accuracy. Another use could be nighttime, all-weather precision bombing. Navstar could also increase dramatically overall U.S. operational capabilities in bad weather. Precision cargo airdrops, rendezvous between aircraft, and certain instrument approaches to landing have already

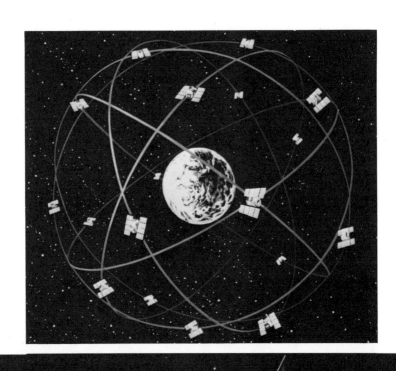

been demonstrated through test satellites in the system. Future uses of Navstar are virtually limitless.

To obtain information from Navstar, a user needs only to push a few buttons on a receiving set. The set will then automatically select the four satellites most favorably located, lock onto their navigational signals, and compute the user's position, velocity, and time. Receiving sets are being developed for integration with aircraft, land vehicles, and ships. A lightweight backpack unit is already under production and being tested for use by ground troops.

There also are numerous civilian applications for Navstar. The Department of Defense is coordinating its activities relating to radio navigational systems with the Department of Transportation, the Federal Aviation Administration, the Department of Commerce, the State Department, and NASA.

Navstar is still in the developmental stage. It could be operational soon.

Above: A new space system, the U.S. Air Force's Navstar Global Positioning System Satellite Constellation, will consist of eighteen Navstar satellites in six circular orbits to enable users worldwide to determine their precise position, velocity, and altitude twenty-four hours a day under any weather conditions.
Below: Artist's concept of a Navstar satellite

T H I R T E E N

SURVEILLANCE SATELLITES

It is an unfortunate fact of the technological times in which we live that powerful, nuclear-armed intercontinental ballistic missiles, aimed at strategic sites in the United States and elsewhere in the Western world, can reach their targets and cause massive destruction within thirty minutes of their launching from platforms deep inside the Soviet Union. The United States, of course, also has the ability to hit Soviet targets within the same short time span by launching its fleets of land- and sea-based nuclear missiles.

A surprise attack on the United States with such awesome weapons could conceivably destroy much of the U.S. retaliatory strike force, crippling military response. At the same time, millions of Americans could be killed. Thus, early warning of such an attack is of paramount importance to the national defense.

For years, the United States relied on high-flying aircraft to supply information on Soviet missile sites and other Soviet military activities. Supersleek jets would fly at heights of 40,000 feet (12,000 m) or more over Soviet territory, photographing ground bases with high resolution photographic equipment.

But such flights had shortcomings. For one thing,

they could not provide around-the-clock coverage. They were also vulnerable to enemy attack. In fact, in 1960 U.S. pilot Francis Gary Powers was shot down over the USSR in his U-2 spy plane. This triggered an international incident, and the Soviets demanded that the United States cease all such missions over their country.

Again, space technology solved the problem. In the early 1960s the air force developed a system to take photographs and gather other intelligence data via satellites in orbit and to retrieve such information for immediate scrutiny on earth. The program was refined over the years, and by the early 1970s the air force had perfected a Satellite Early-Warning System (SEWS) to keep watch on the world.

At first, two satellites were deployed in geosynchronous orbit, 22,300 miles (35,900 km) up. One was placed over the Indian Ocean to monitor land-based missile sites in the Soviet Union. The other was strategically placed at a point high over Panama to monitor any sea-launched ballistic missiles in the Atlantic or Pacific oceans.

Not only were these electronic "spies" in space instantly able to spot any missile launchings from foreign sites, but they could also project the point of impact of any ICBM within one minute from the time of its launch. Additionally, they could detect and report any nuclear explosions in the atmosphere.

Had the United States, for example, had surveillance satellites operating in space in December 1941, the surprise attack on Pearl Harbor by the Japanese might not have been possible. Data from space would have reported the massing of the Japanese fleet off Hawaii in ample time for defensive countermeasures to have been taken.

Photographic reconnaissance satellites serve two complementary missions: They take panoramic photographs from earth orbit to uncover evidence of new military installations under construction—installations such as airfields or missile sites—and they are also used to obtain high-resolution pictures of specific existing installations. Camera and sensing systems aboard these "spy" satellites are capable of photographing details of 12-inch-high (.3-m) objects from orbital distances of several hundred miles. They orbit the earth every ninety minutes, and by changing their orbit they can pass over the total global surface of the planet twice daily, once in daylight and once in darkness.

To detect the launching of foreign missiles, surveillance satellites have one sensor that can detect and report infrared (heat) emissions given off by a rocket's engines and a second that can record the rise of a rocket into the atmosphere by tracing light reflections. Signals from these satellites are relayed automatically to ground receivers, then beamed via communications satellites to the North American Air Defense Command (NORAD) control center near Colorado Springs, Colorado. At this command post are computers of such sophistication and speed that they can analyze the flight characteristics of an object in space and tell where it originated and if its purpose is peaceful—all in a fraction of a second.

To obtain maximum clarity in the pictures sent by photo-reconnaissance satellites, the pictures are not transmitted electronically, as sensor data is, but are recovered from orbit, then processed. To get them back to earth, a technique similar to the one used by NASA to return American astronauts from early space flights is employed, but with one important difference: When the spacecraft has used up its film, after a few weeks or months in orbit, a capsule containing the photographs is ejected upon radio command as the satellite passes over Alaska. The capsule then follows a ballistic trajectory toward Hawaii until it reaches an altitude of approximately 50,000 feet (15,000 m), at which time parachutes are released. But instead of descending to the ocean surface, as the early astronauts did, the capsule is recovered in midair by a C-130 aircraft.

Guided by ground radar and a radio signal from the capsule itself, the C-130 crew snags the cargo and hauls it aboard. The capsule is designed to be able to remain afloat in the ocean for a period of twenty-four hours, to enable U.S. frogmen to retrieve it in case a catch is missed. The satellite, now useless, soon reenters the earth's atmosphere and is burned up.

In the mid-1970s, the early reconnaissance satellites were replaced by a new, larger, more powerful, and more sophisticated series nicknamed "Big Bird." Big Bird is a 12-ton, 55-foot-long (16.5-m) technological marvel that carries electronic listening gear along with black and white, color, and infrared television and still cameras. The satellite not only provides detailed data on Soviet and Chinese military movements and missile locations, but also charts other information such as grain harvests. Exposed film shot on these orbital missions is periodically parachuted to earth, where it is snagged in midair over the Pacific by specially equipped air force planes. It then is speeded to military intelligence centers for immediate analysis.

Until recent years, U.S. surveillance satellites were somewhat limited in what they could cover by the weather. On cloudless days, they could operate perfectly and their photographs and television images were sharp enough to read the license plates on cars parked in Moscow. However, Eastern Europe is covered with clouds two-thirds of the time, which greatly hampered timely intelligence operations.

But the newest U.S. satellites can form images in infrared light and have the capability of taking photographs at night as well as through cloud cover. A new type of radar is being developed, too, that can form sharp images of terrain completely covered by clouds.

Spaceborne early-warning systems are backed up by a

network of ground-based radar instruments that can identify electrified particles, or ions, left in the atmosphere by rocket launches. Ground-based instruments also keep track of all artificial objects in space. One ground-based early-warning system is called PAVE PAWS. It consists of a pair of solid-state radar systems, one on each coast of the continental United States.

In the event of an enemy launch of intercontinental ballistic missiles, these giant, ground-based radar installations would tell the potential numbers and destinations of the missiles. This vital information would then be simultaneously passed to the National Command Authorities in Washington, D.C., to the North American Air Defense Command in Colorado, and to the Strategic Air Command.

PAVE PAWS also has the ability to track and display data on the position and velocity of hundreds of satellites orbiting the earth. Using what is called "phased-array" technology, the system can track more targets more accurately than ever before and at greater range, while at the same time using less power. "Phased array" means that the PAVE PAWS "eyes" are steered electronically, using thousands of small radar antennas coordinated by two large computers. Since no mechanical parts limit the speed of the radar scan, it can rapidly detect and locate orbiting objects. Its computers also allow it to automatically detect, track, and predict the impact point of an enemy missile.

Because it is very important to the Defense Department to know exactly what is in space—where objects are and where they are going—the air force is working on a new program to complement the PAVE PAWS system. Using the latest in silicon-chip technology, the Air Force Systems Command is developing a worldwide network of monitoring stations to improve on U.S. ability to identify and track orbiting objects. Known as GEODSS, for *G*round-based *E*lectro-*O*ptical *D*eep *S*pace *S*urveillance, this network will consist of installations at five widely scattered sites—at the White Sands Missile Range in New Mexico and in South Korea, Hawaii, the Indian Ocean, and in an eastern Atlantic region.

Equipped with powerful telescopes, these installations will relay images from objects in space onto photo-imaging tubes, which will then convert the picture to electronic pulses. These pulses will then be fed into computers and the data obtained sent to air force master computers, where all objects in space are monitored constantly. GEODSS will be able to spot an object in space the size of a soccer ball at a distance of 25,000 miles (40,000 km). The system was planned to be completely operational by 1987.

The Defense Advanced Research Projects Agency (DARPA) is also looking into the feasibility of developing active space-based radar systems. Such satellites would provide all-weather capabilities and accurate target-range information crucial for many strategic missions. The primary goals of this program are improved radar devices and ways to spread the radar functions over several satellites to increase the system's survivability. Agency experts say this program would have major impact on a range of military missions, including air vehicle surveillance, and, if successful, could negate the need for large networks of ground-based radar installations.

Of course, the Soviets, too, have developed a highly refined series of satellites to support their military operations. They have launched hundreds of surveillance satellites over the past twenty years to keep orbital watch on U.S. military sites and other military activites in this country and in other areas of the world.

But there is an irony here. The Soviet Union has always been much more secretive about its military installations and activities than the United States has. But when it launched the first satellite into orbit, *Sput-*

nik, in 1957, it did so without first obtaining approval for it to fly over other nations. This established the principle that a country's domain does not extend to outer space as it does to air-space at lower altitudes. So today, although the Russians may complain about having their land constantly surveyed by satellites, it is they who set the precedent.

In the past few years, early-warning and surveillance satellites have become a vital part of the U.S. national defense. Not only are they capable of detecting the launching of enemy missiles, giving the United States time to prepare and to strike back, but they also furnish important information on day-to-day military activities around the world. And they provide a means of verifying that nations live up to arms-limitation agreements. In effect, these satellites may have considerably diminished the danger of war by enabling the major nuclear powers to keep a close check on each other's military installations.

As early as 1967, President Lyndon B. Johnson acknowledged the significance of such a spatial surveillance system when he said in a speech: "We've spent $35 to $40 billion on the space program [including the Apollo moon project]. And if nothing else had come out of it except the knowledge we've gained from space photography, it would be worth ten times what the whole program has cost. Because . . . we know how many missiles the enemy has. And it turns out, our [previous] guesses were way off. We were doing things we didn't need to do. We were building things we didn't need to build. We were harboring fears we didn't need to harbor."

More than ten years later, President Jimmy Carter would add: "Photo reconnaissance satellites have become an important stabilizing factor in world affairs. In the monitoring of arms-control agreements, they make an immense contribution to the security of all nations. We shall continue to develop them."

F O U R T E E N

THE ALL-PURPOSE SHUTTLE

The placement of military and civilian satellites into orbit is an extremely expensive venture. Booster rockets alone, with their powerful engines, cost millions of dollars and are used just once. Then, after their payload has been rocketed into space, they are jettisoned and land somewhere in the ocean, ruined and usually lost forever. Commenting on this, Dr. Kurt H. Debus, former director of NASA's Kennedy Space Center in Florida, where most U.S. launches take place, said: "Business does not discard a Greyhound bus after its first trip from New York to Miami. But that, in effect, is what NASA and the Department of Defense must do every time a space mission is launched with conventional rockets."

The spacecrafts themselves are enormously expensive, too. They must be designed for complex operations, yet be lightweight. And once they have been flown into orbit, if even the tiniest part malfunctions, it can cause the whole satellite to shut down, rendering the mission a failure. Even satellites that work as planned eventually stop functioning, only to continue circling the earth as useless pieces of metallic junk. All these objects must be replaced by new satellites launched by new rockets.

In the early 1970s, a special Space Task Group was

assembled to come up with suggestions for a new, more efficient space transportation system. The group recommended that the United States develop a system that would "carry passengers, supplies, rocket fuel, other spacecraft, equipment, or additional rocket stages to and from orbit on a routine, aircraftlike basis."[12]

The concept of America's space shuttle was born.

Endorsing the recommendation of the group, President Richard M. Nixon, on January 5, 1972, said:

The United States should proceed at once with the development of an entirely new type of space transportation system [STS] designed to help transform the space frontier of the 1970s into familiar territory, easily accessible for human endeavor in the 1980s and 1990s.

The system will center on a space vehicle that can shuttle repeatedly from earth to orbit and back. . . . It will go a long way toward delivering the rich benefits of practical space use and the valuable spin-offs from space efforts into the daily lives of Americans and all people. The space shuttle program is the right next step for America to take, in moving out from our present beachhead in the sky to achieve a real working presence in space. [The shuttle] will make the ride safer and less demanding for the passengers, so that men and women with work to do in space can commute aloft, without having to spend years in training.

NASA was chosen as the agency to design, build, and fly the shuttle.

After several years of conducting its own studies, the air force, also in the early 1970s, concluded that the most promising way to cut costs significantly in space would be through the use of reusable launch vehicles. These studies further pointed out that additional savings could be made by being able to recover and reuse satellites and to conduct in-orbit maintenance on those systems that developed defects.[13]

At that point it seemed logical for the military to join NASA in its efforts to build the space shuttle. From the earliest design stages of the shuttle program, air force experts worked very closely with NASA and with industry engineers and technicians to help define a system that would meet defense requirements in addition to the requirements needed for civilian missions.

The air force also pledged full support of the program, offering its years of aerospace expertise that had been developed and refined through the testing, launching, and operation of hundreds of large aircraft, missiles, rockets, and spacecraft. Much of this expertise could be directly applied to the shuttle, which was to be flown and operated much like a large aircraft.

The Defense Department projected that up to a third or more of all shuttle missions would be devoted to military purposes. Although some people objected to this, insisting that NASA was charged with the peaceful use of space only, without the financial support of the air force it is doubtful that NASA would have received anywhere near enough funding to build the shuttle at all.

The space shuttle orbiter resembles a large aircraft with stubby delta wings. It is 122 feet (36.6 m) long and has a 78-foot (23.4-m) wingspan. In addition to the orbiter, the vehicle has a large external liquid fuel tank and two smaller solid-fuel rocket boosters. When launched into space, the large missile-shaped external tank, which contains liquid hydrogen and oxygen for the orbiter's main engines, is attached to the orbiter. The rocket boosters are attached to the large external tank.

About two minutes after lift-off, at an altitude of about 27 miles (43.2 km), the boosters burn out and separate from the orbiter. These are then parachuted into the ocean to be recovered, refurbished, and reused. The main engines of the orbiter continue to burn until the external tank is almost empty. Then the tank separates and burns up or breaks apart upon reentry into the earth's atmosphere. The external tank is the only part of the shuttle vehicle's three main elements that was not designed to be reusable. At this point the orbiter continues on independently, and goes into low earth orbit, using its orbital maneuvering system engines. Once in orbit the crew can begin the mission's assigned tasks.

After completion of its mission—lasting anywhere from a week to a month or more in orbit—the shuttle reenters the atmosphere. Automatic systems then guide it to an unpowered landing, as if it were a huge, high-speed glider. The shuttle is the first manned spacecraft designed to touch down on a landing strip.

Not only is the shuttle designed to cut down greatly on launch costs, but it also performs a variety of jobs in space more efficiently and less expensively than was previously possible. For example, in a study of 131 satellite failures over a period of years, 78 were found to be related to faulty launches. Others involved faulty spacecraft payloads that either didn't work once they were in orbit or worked poorly and could have been repaired in space or returned to earth for repair if the shuttle had been available to service or retrieve them.

Such maintenance and repair jobs in orbit are only one of the many functions the shuttle carries out. Its designed versatility, in fact, is one of the most important selling points of the program.

In a sense, the orbiter serves as a sort of "space truck," hauling satellites to be placed into earth orbit. At least five different satellites may be carried up at one time. Each is carefully examined before it is loaded aboard the orbiter. Once in orbit, the shuttle crew gives the satellite a final going over. After determining that everything is still working properly, the crew operates the payload-deployment system. This spindly mechanical arm, working like a giant crane, lifts the satellite from the cargo bay, moves it away from the orbiter, and releases it. Final activation of the satellite is by radio command, but the orbiter and crew stay near the satellite until they are sure it is operating satisfactorily.

This type of satellite placement saves millions of dollars a year over present systems. For one thing, current satellites have to be designed with expensive backup parts for much of their critical equipment, so that if one part fails in space, the backup part is activated. With the shuttle standing by, however, such duplication becomes unnecessary. If the satellite does not start performing properly, it can be retrieved and taken back to earth for necessary repairs.

Also, with satellites today, many of their systems, including their computers, experiment packages, sensors, and so on, have to be miniaturized at additional expense to fit within extremely tight weight limitations. This is greatly relaxed on the shuttle, which can comfortably carry much heavier payloads into space.

Cost savings can also be made by refurbishing satellites rather than having to build new ones for each mission. If a satellite fails in low earth orbit, or if it simply stops operating, the orbiter will rendezvous with it in space, and its remote manipulator arm will reach out and grab the satellite, which will then be lowered into the cargo bay and locked into place for the return trip home. On earth, engineers can repair any malfunctioning parts or reequip the satellite with fresh systems and parts. It can then be returned on a later shuttle flight to its position in orbit.

In addition to the ferrying of satellites and spacecraft to and from orbit, the shuttle also has the ability to place large, free-flying objects in space, such as laboratories for scientific purposes, military command posts, or telescopes. Astronauts or other crew members on the shuttle are able to "walk" in space. On such excursions they might install or remove film cassettes, material samples, protective covers, and instruments; operate equipment such as assembly tools, sensors, and cleaning devices; repair, replace, calibrate, reposition, and inspect equipment; and adjust antennas or instruments on the satellite or payload.

Although the shuttle is extremely versatile as a space transportation system, it does have its limitations. Its design restricts it to low-altitude, near-earth orbital flights. Many satellites today, and about half of those planned for the future, must achieve much higher orbits to do their jobs effectively. Communications satellites, for example, must be placed in a geosynchronous orbit, 22,300 miles (35,680 km) above the earth, to operate effectively.

Other satellites must be launched into highly elliptical orbits, with wide-ranging arcs that swing near the earth at times, then travel many miles away. Also, some satellites or space probes are intended to go into orbit around neighboring planets, or to venture deep into the solar system and beyond.

For these higher orbital flights and deep-space probes, the shuttle can carry both satellite and propulsion systems, or engines, into earth orbit. There, they will be deployed much like other payloads. Once in orbit the entire system—satellite and propulsion package—is thoroughly checked over and readied for its final launch. Guidance information is updated. The orbiter then moves to a safe distance away before ground control gives the radio command to fire the engines that will boost the satellite or probe toward its ultimate destination.

A propulsion stage, called the inertial upper stage, or IUS, using solid rocket fuel is being developed by the Department of Defense and will be used in such orbital launches. Although the military services have many uses for high-orbit space hardware, NASA, too, will be a major user. The air force is working with NASA and other potential users to design the IUS to meet all future requirements, military and civilian.

The shuttle was designed to be capable of being launched either from the East Coast of the United States, at NASA's Kennedy Space Center, or from the West Coast, at Vandenberg Air Force Base in California, between Los Angeles and San Francisco. The majority of missions from Kennedy are for satellites and spacecraft that operate in orbits around or near the equator. Flights from Vandenberg are made to place satellites in polar orbit. Such orbits cover more square miles of the earth and are used for such missions as the Landsat earth-resource surveillance program and DOD missions.

It is safer to launch into polar orbit from the West Coast. To reach polar orbit from the Kennedy Center would require the shuttle to fly over populated areas, such as Cuba, enroute to space. NASA prefers to fly over water only wherever possible. This can be achieved from Vandenberg out over the Pacific Ocean. Launches for other orbital flights can be made from Kennedy without flying over land.

As routine access to space becomes a reality, the way will be opened to what the air force calls "a new generation of practical military use of space." The shuttle can deliver more usable hardware than is possible with existing boosters. Greater payload capacity brings with it greater reliability, made possible by the addition of backup systems and subsystems. Military needs cannot tolerate loss of vital services due to equipment failure. The more trustworthy space systems are, the better the air force can carry out its mission of defending the United States against attacks from or through space.

Further into the future, the air force envisions "huge structures" that can be built in space to provide solar and nuclear power for military and civilian uses. New manufacturing techniques in the near-zero gravity of space may make possible the creation of entirely new materials of higher purity and strength that could have significant economic and military impact. Another possibility in which the air force is keenly interested is the development of a spaceborne command post, providing better command, control, and communications, with less vulnerability to attack.

Of course, to have a military expert or team of

experts aboard a spacecraft in earth orbit would offer enormous advantages. The time-honored military tradition of sending scouts out to see where the enemy is and what they are doing would reach its ultimate application, since an orbital vantage point would encompass the entire world below. Such experts could also verify and confirm the findings of surveillance satellites and other space instrumentation and act upon the data instantly, thereby reducing the hazard of responding to a false threat, such as a signal indicating a foreign missile launching or nuclear blast, which has in reality been caused by equipment malfunction.

A person aboard the shuttle could spot an enemy missile or satellite and aim a knockout weapon at it faster and with greater accuracy than a land-based individual. He or she could also direct sensors at likely reconnaissance targets and could sift out irrelevant data and relay only important information to earth.

The air force, in fact, has long considered the possibilities of either placing its experts aboard the shuttle on a full-time basis or taking control of the shuttle altogether at some point in the future. This topic has been under active consideration for at least ten years. In 1972, for example, Grant Hansen, then assistant secretary of the air force, said: "Operation of the shuttle by the air force in the manner of a Military Airlift Command for space operations . . . is an arrangement which would go into effect only after the operation of the shuttle has matured to a routine basis.

"NASA management may not be opposed to the eventual transfer of shuttle operation to the air force, because its primary interests are in research and development, and not in the field of operations," Hansen said. "Of course, some consideration has been given to NASA operating the system on a permanent basis, but the fact that in the event of war the system might have to be operated by the military weighs against such an approach."

F I F T E E N

AFTER THE *CHALLENGER*

On January 28, 1986, the space shuttle *Challenger* was destroyed when a giant rocket booster tank exploded during flight, a little more than a minute after lift-off from the Kennedy Space Center in Florida. The entire crew of seven, including New Hampshire schoolteacher Christa McAuliffe, was instantly killed.

An investigation was launched soon after to find the cause of the spectacular accident. Future shuttle flights were postponed indefinitely, and, in a sense, the whole U.S. space program was put on "temporary hold."

President Ronald Reagan put the *Challenger* disaster in perspective as well as anyone when, speaking of the astronauts, he said, "They had a hunger to explore the universe and discover its truths. . . . They served all of us." Then, talking specifically to the nation's students, he said, "I know it's hard to understand that sometimes painful things like this happen. It's all part of the process of exploration and discovery, it's all part of taking a chance and expanding man's horizons."

The president left no doubt as to America's future course in space, however. "We'll continue our quest in space," he said. "There will be more shuttle flights and more shuttle crews." William Graham, NASA's acting administrator, added: "The space shuttle is our principal space transportation system; it will remain our principal space transportation system for the foreseeable future."

After several months of exhaustive investigations, it was determined that faulty seals in the shuttle's solid rocket booster engines had malfunctioned, leading to the explosion. NASA was given the charge to completely redesign these engines—a task estimated to take a year or longer.

Meanwhile, in April 1986, the air force awarded contracts worth between $300 and $400 million to industries for the development of a new aerospace plane. This is to be equipped with scramjet engines that burn their fuel in an airstream that moves at supersonic speeds. The plane is expected to be capable of taking off from a runway and quickly acclerating to speeds twelve to twenty-five times the speed of sound.

With the aid of a built-in rocket, the plane could climb above the atmosphere and into a low orbit of earth. Planners for both the military and NASA see the aerospace plane as becoming a more versatile, efficient, and lower-cost means of delivering people and payloads to space than conventional rockets or the shuttle.

President Reagan has endorsed the program, although the first flight tests probably won't occur until the early 1990s.

For the more near-term future, it appears a redesigned shuttle will carry the bulk of the load, augmented by unmanned rockets. And a large percentage of the missions will continue to be military, beginning again in the late 1980s.

S I X T E E N

SPACE TREATIES

The most sane and sensible way to halt the weapons race in space, thereby curbing the enormous costs such a race involves and at the same time greatly reducing the chances of a cataclysmic war breaking out, is through peaceful negotiations leading to the eventual banning of all such systems. If the United States and the Soviet Union could agree on such a treaty, there would be no need for either side, or any other nation, to spend another penny for the development of offensive or defensive weapons systems in space.

The two nations have made proposals and counter-proposals for limiting the development of their military space programs for the last quarter-century, generally with disappointing results. The United Nations is also deeply involved in this effort but has had only marginal success. Negotiating such treaties is a highly complicated and often frustrating business and has been from the start.

As early as 1958, for example, the year after *Sputnik* opened the space age, the Soviet Union at the United Nations called for "the banning of the use of cosmic space for military purposes." But the United States and a number of other nations objected to certain provisions in this proposal. The Russians also asked in 1958 for creation of an international agency for the scientific exploration of space. But this was withdrawn a year later when the Soviets landed a space probe on the moon and Premier Nikita Khrushchev claimed the entire moon as Soviet territory.

In 1960, U.S. President Dwight D. Eisenhower, speaking at the UN's General Assembly, suggested that outer space be treated as Antarctica is under the Antarctic Treaty. Most nations quickly agreed to the proposal keeping Antarctica, a virgin continent, a neutral zone free of weapons of any kind.

The Antarctic Treaty provides that Antarctica shall be used for peaceful purposes only. It specifically prohibits any "measures of a military nature, such as the establishment of military bases and fortifications, the carrying out of military manuevers, as well as the testing of any types of weapons." Nuclear explosions and the disposal of radioactive wastes there are also forbidden. Further, it was agreed that all treaty-signing nations would have free access at any time to all parts of the continent and could send observers at any time to inspect installations to make sure they were not being used for military purposes.

The Antarctic Treaty has worked well for more than twenty years. One reason for this, experts feel, is that it is much easier to exclude armaments than it is to eliminate or control them once they have been introduced into an area. President Eisenhower thought this concept could be applied to space as well, since, at that time, there were no weapons in space. The Soviets, too, seemed in agreement, but negotiations proceeded slowly, hit many technical snags, and no significant progress could be made.

The United Nations continued to work diligently toward the resolution of problems, and finally, in October 1967—ten years after the *Sputnik* launch—the Outer Space Treaty was ratified. It contains two important provisions. First, it says that nations are "not to place in orbit around the earth, install on the moon or any other celestial body, or otherwise station in outer space, nuclear or any other weapons of mass destruction."

Second, it "limits the use of the moon and other celestial bodies exclusively to peaceful purposes and expressly prohibits their use for establishing military bases, installations or fortifications; testing weapons of any kind; or conducting military maneuvers."

Although this treaty was a big step in the right direction, many felt it did not go far enough—that it should have barred the use of space for any military purposes. For example, it covered nuclear but not conventional weapons. Some also believed there were too many loopholes in the agreement, which would tend to encourage further militaristic developments. One provision stated: "The use of military personnel for scientific research or any other peaceful purposes shall *not* be prohibited."

Consequently, it was determined that the launching of satellites into earth orbit for such defense missions as communications, weather observations, navigation, surveillance, and early warning could continue. It was argued that photo-reconnaissance satellites are important in their use to verify that nations are following arms-control agreements, and therefore they are, in reality, serving peaceful tasks. In 1972, the Antiballistic Missile Treaty specifically prohibited interference with a nation's use of technical means to verify treaty provisions.

Two years later, the UN General Assembly adopted a resolution requiring registration of objects launched into outer space. The United Nations said such a system would "assist in the identification of such objects, and would contribute to the application and development of international law governing the exploration and use of outer space."

Article II of this agreement states: "When a space

object is launched into earth orbit or beyond, the launching State shall register the space object by means of an entry in an appropriate registry which it shall maintain. Each launching State shall inform the Secretary-General of the United Nations of the establishment of such a registry." Article IV says that the United Nations should be informed of the "general function of the space object."

In December 1979, the United Nations went further in spelling out restrictions on the military uses of the moon by issuing a resolution adopted by the General Assembly. Article III of this "Agreement governing the activities of States on the moon and other celestial bodies" states:

The moon [and other celestial bodies] shall be used by all States Parties exclusively for peaceful purposes.

Any threat or use of force or any other hostile act or threat of hostile act on the moon is prohibited. It is likewise prohibited to use the moon in order to commit any such act or to engage in any such threat in relation to the earth, the moon, spacecraft, the personnel of spacecraft or man-made space objects.

States Parties shall not place in orbit around or other trajectory to or around the moon objects carrying nuclear weapons or any other kinds of weapons of mass destruction or place or use such weapons on or in the moon.

The establishment of military bases, installations and fortifications, the testing of any type of weapons and the conduct of military maneuvers on the moon shall be forbidden.

Having such treaties on the books is one thing. Enforcing them is another. It became quite clear that the Soviets, in testing a new series of antisatellite weapons systems in the early 1970s, were violating the tenets of the Outer Space Treaty of 1967. Protests were raised against this action, but the Soviets continued their testing, obviously aimed at developing the ability to destroy foreign spacecraft in earth orbit.

The United States at the same time was not developing such a capability, and this presented a problem to the Department of Defense. The U.S. Arms Control and Disarmament Agency, in its 1980 report to the president of the United States, addressed this point: "Because of the growing importance of both civilian and military satellites, the prospect of systems that could threaten satellites has given rise to serious concern. . . . Development of antisatellite systems by one side would likely lead to development of such systems by the other to avoid its being placed at a significant disadvantage. Development of such systems would also call into question the ability of satellites in their vital missions to provide strategic warning or to carry out other functions in time of conflict."

Early in 1978 President Jimmy Carter urged the Soviet Union to begin negotiations on banning "killer" satellites. The Defense Department objected to this, because they believed the Russians already had a workable antisatellite system, while the United States did not. The Defense Department was in the early stages of building two different antisatellite systems. They were also undertaking a number of programs to reduce the vulnerability of U.S. satellites to attack. Military experts believed that if an agreement was reached banning such systems, it would put the United States at a disadvantage because the Russians already had such a system and could deploy it in time of crisis or war, whereas the United States still needed to develop its systems. Officials also acknowledged that a simple ban on the deployment of killer satellites would be extremely difficult to enforce, partly because it would be hard to distinguish this type of satellite from others used for peaceful missions.

Nevertheless, talks began in Helsinki, Finland, in

June 1978. Two additional sessions were held in 1979, one in Bern, Switzerland, and the other in Vienna, Austria. According to the U.S. Arms Control and Disarmament Agency, "progress was made in these discussions, but important issues still remain to be solved." The U.S.–Soviet joint communique issued at the Vienna talks stated that the sides "agreed to continue actively searching for a mutually acceptable agreement in the continuing negotiations on antisatellite systems."

However, the Soviets set several conditions at these first sessions that the United States found unacceptable. The key problem revolved around the use of the American space shuttle. The Soviet negotiators wanted the United States to scrap the space shuttle program entirely, or at least pledge not to use the vehicle for military purposes. In fact, the Russians had stated from the day the first shuttle was launched that they believed the United States intended to use the shuttle as a battle-station command post in space. United States negotiators refused to even discuss this demand, and no agreement could be reached.

In December 1979, preparations were under way for a fourth round of talks, when the Soviet Union invaded Afghanistan. In response to the Soviet action, the United States broke off all talks. Four months later the Russians resumed their killer-satellite testing program with the launching of *Cosmos 1174*, a newer, more advanced system. Meanwhile, the United States stepped up its development of an antisatellite program.

Thus, for the time being at least, the hope of preventing an escalation of the space-weapons race through peaceful negotiations has been sidetracked. Yet many experts believe that any move toward further talks must come quickly, before advanced space-weapons systems now on the drawing boards and in laboratories become reality. If technology moves faster than limitations talks, there will be little hope for a settlement.

To date, both the United States and the Soviet Union have concentrated on specific details of space weaponry in their discussions. Some officials feel this has been a mistake—that future talks should focus on actions, not devices. They contend that by banning the testing as well as the deployment of space-based systems, the superpowers would be able to arrive at an agreement acceptable to both.

For example, ground-based testing of laser devices intended for use in space could conceivably be concealed, but space-based testing of such systems could not. And such a weapon, involving advanced technology, could not become a useful operational tool without extensive testing in space. An agreement that prohibited space-based testing could relieve Soviet apprehensions about the space shuttle and at the same time quell United States fears concerning the intended use of large space stations the Soviets are planning.

In any case, the time for action on a weapons-banning treaty in space seems to be now, before such systems can be refined and placed in orbit. Once they are in orbit, any chance of agreement on a meaningful policy will be greatly reduced, or more likely, irretrievably lost.

S E V E N T E E N

THE SOVIET PROGRAM

The Soviet Union has been dead set against America's Strategic Defense Initiative ever since it was first publicly announced in 1983. According to Soviet officials, if the United States builds a defense against Soviet nuclear attacks, the United States might then attack the USSR, knowing it would be protected against Soviet retaliation. Some U.S. critics of SDI have even gone as far as saying the Soviets might feel so threatened by this possibility that they could launch a missile attack on the United States just to keep us from building the system.

This line of reasoning assumes that in the future the United States will have a space- and ground-based defense against Soviet ICBMs, but that the Soviets would have no such defense against U.S. ballistic missiles. This is a false assumption.

As space expert Dr. Robert Jastrow said, ". . . the Soviets are working as hard as they can on their own missile defense program, and have been for more than a decade. If one country gets a missile defense before the other, it will be the Soviet Union that does so and not the United States."[14]

Former U.S. Secretary of Defense Caspar Weinberger has said the entire Soviet space program, including the development of weapons and the building of a missile defense system, is ten times the size of America's effort. Experts say the Soviets are, and have been, pouring enormous amounts of money into a space defense system, and that they now have a beam-weapons research program two to three times as large as that of the United States. They were the first to test a beam weapon, back in 1969.

Dr. Jastrow says the Soviet Union has been testing its defenses against American missiles ever since it signed the ABM treaty. In 1973, the Russians began to test their surface-to-air missiles at altitudes close to 100,000 feet (30,000 m). Since no aircraft fly at this exalted height, it is safe to assume they were working on an anti-missile system. More recently, the Soviets unveiled a newer, faster surface-to-air missile, the SA-12, which travels at 12,000 miles (19,000 km) per hour—the same speed as nuclear ballistic missiles.

But the Russians are known to have been working on weapons systems in space—offensive, not defensive—more than twenty years ago. For example, they are known to have been developing a working killer satellite since the mid-1960s (see chapter 18).

As early as 1966, a year before the Outer Space Treaty was signed, banning the use of nuclear weapons in space, the Soviet Union began testing an ominous system called the Fractional Orbital Bombardment System, or FOBS, designed to launch giant rockets armed with nuclear warheads into orbit about 100 miles (160 km) above the earth. From such a vantage point, these warheads could be dispatched at hypersonic speeds (five times the speed of sound) through space and back into the earth's atmosphere, toward virtually any target on the planet.

According to U.S. intelligence sources, from 1966 through 1971 at least eighteen FOBS tests were conducted by the Soviets. It is believed that many of the earlier tests ended in failure, although some of the later ones were probably successful.

The Russians are also believed to have tested a system called the Multiple Orbital Bombardment System (MOBS), whereby bomb-carrying satellites completed several orbits before they were brought down. In times of international tension, a ring of such satellites could be placed around the earth, and, theoretically at least, be launched from orbit at any time to rain terror down on earth targets.

A Congressional report, prepared in 1979 for the U.S. House of Representatives Subcommittee on Space Science and Applications, warned: "From a Soviet point of view, FOBS has the advantage of complicating U.S. defenses. Although scientifically speaking the warhead is in orbit, in effect it is like an extended-range ICBM capable of flying the long way around the world to bypass the normal ballistic missile early-warning system (BMEWS) radar defenses which point to the north.

"But such flights in combat have disadvantages, too," the report said, "including reduced accuracy on target if coming in the long way around, and reduced payload by any route compared with the use of the same launch vehicle as an ICBM."

Despite the obvious disadvantages, the Russians apparently felt that the development of a FOBS system was worth the effort. In fact, the normally highly secretive Soviets even bragged about it. Radio Moscow said, "There is no limit to the range of FOBS," and "the main property of weapons of this class is their ability to hit enemy objectives literally from any direction, which makes them virtually invulnerable to antimissile defense means."

Mysteriously, the Russians stopped FOBS test flights in 1971. In summarizing the situation, the congressional report to the House subcommittee said: "The United States does not have a FOBS program because it does not regard it as necessary or desirable. The Russians obviously do, or did, for reasons not wholly clear."

The Soviets also are known to have the only operational ballistic missile defense system in existence today. It is called the Galosh antiballistic missile, and large numbers of these weapons are set up ringing the city of Moscow. They also have developed mobile antiballistic missile radars and missiles located at ICBM sites all around the Soviet Union.

In combination with their illegal radars, which violate the ABM treaty, these missiles and radars could give the Russians a crude nationwide ABM capability by the 1990s. Experts say it would not be enough to defend against an all-out U.S. first strike, but it might provide a sufficient defense against a counterstrike by a weakened U.S. arsenal.

Today, Soviet research on lasers and other advanced Star Wars weapons is going full blast. NASA head Dr. James Fletcher, who directed a study of missile defense, says there is "striking evidence that the Soviet Union has pursued with vigor all the [missile defense] technologies we have recommended [for the United States] and many which we do not even understand yet. . . . The Soviet Union is pursuing their [Star Wars] program at the fastest pace their technology allows. It is unlikely that they could accelerate their effort more than they have, whatever we do."[15]

Some United States experts say if the Russians do build a Star Wars-type defense similar to the one being developed by the United Staes, it is not necessarily such a bad thing. Says Dr. Jastrow: "No development could be more favorable to the cause of ending the nuclear arms race and eliminating nuclear weapons from the world. . . . If both the United States and USSR put a defense against missiles in place, neither country will be able to overwhelm the other's defense by building more missiles, and both nations must then recognize the futility of a continued competition in the building of offensive weapons of mass destruction."

– 103

E I G H T E E N

KILLER SATELLITES

At T-minus zero hour on December 3, 1971, huge reddish-orange tongues of flame shot out of the great rocket's tail at the secret Soviet launch base in Tyuratam, in South Central Asia. Minutes later the booster had ejected its payload—a satellite designated *Cosmos 462*—into earth orbit.

By ground control, the mysterious spacecraft was skillfully jockeyed from one orbit to another, finally settling into one 150 miles (240 km) above the planet. Then it was put on the trail of *Cosmos 459*, another Russian satellite that had been launched four days earlier. Swiftly and surely, like a sharp-eyed electronic hawk with its prey in sight, *Cosmos 462* homed in on its sister ship. It closed to within point-blank range. The two craft flew side by side, in tandem, for a brief period.

Then suddenly, without warning, the eerie calm of space was shattered with a frightening explosion that instantly demolished both Cosmos vehicles, ripping them into useless, jagged metallic shreds that went flying off in a dozen directions. Both vehicles were destroyed within the flash of a single pulsed signal.

The mission was successful. *Cosmos 462* had been a killer satellite, designed to seek out and destroy *Cosmos*

459 in earth orbit. The Russians secretly hailed the mission. U.S. military officials were deeply concerned. Not only was this still another in a series of test flights obviously designed to perfect a spatial weapons system, but *Cosmos 462*'s success also demonstrated that the Soviets now had the ability to blast objects out of near-earth orbit, 100 to 150 miles (160 to 240 km) up. This was about the same altitude at which most of America's surveillance satellites then flew.

In two similar tests earlier in the year, Cosmos interceptors blew up close to target spacecraft flying at higher altitudes, 360 to 550 miles (580 to 880 km) up, on paths similar to those flown by early U.S. communications and navigational satellites. The more recent test showed that the Russians had apparently perfected interception at the lower altitude—a major technological advance, since the nearer the earth, the faster the target moves in relation to the ground below.

The Soviets did not announce the mission of *Cosmos 462*. But by this time, with improved tracking and the help of intelligence sources, American experts could identify individual missions by analyzing the orbital path, the launching site, the altitude, the length of time in orbit, and other signs. When *Cosmos 462* was launched, for example, a U.S. surveillance satellite detected the exhaust gases of the rising rocket and relayed the information instantly to ground stations, which began tracking the payload when it reached orbit. Within minutes after it had exploded near its target, the trackers knew that it had blown to pieces.

Two months after the launch of *Cosmos 462*, a U.S. report on the Soviet space program disclosed that the Russians had, since 1967, launched at least eighteen spacecraft aimed at developing a satellite-destroyer program. The report indicated that the Russians had deliberately blown up at least seven orbital payloads in tests of the system.

The report said further: "The Russians were aware that at one point the United States had had an unmanned system called 'Saint,' which was supposed to co-orbit with potentially dangerous foreign satellites and inspect them. This program was abandoned by the United States.

"It now seems a reasonable inference that the Soviet Union has actively pursued and possibly perfected a system which is capable of reaching a co-orbit with another satellite which is uncooperative, making some kind of an inspection, and if [it is decided that] it is hostile, destroying it."

The report warned: "If Soviet space capabilities grow sufficiently in relation to those of the United States, there is the potential risk that space will become an active arena of conflict even if weapons of mass destruction are not employed in violation of existing treaties."

It was at this time, in 1972, that the Soviets halted testing of their killer-satellite program. But they resumed it in February 1976, confusing U.S. military officials. "We thought they had stopped their ASAT [antisatellite] program," admitted one high-ranking expert. "Instead, they just went home and cleaned up the system, because we've seen improved kill capability."

Proving this point, the Soviets launched *Cosmos 970* into low earth orbit in December 1977. Before it had circled the globe once, it was shifted by ground command into a path ranging from approximately 588 to 712 miles (940.8 to 1,139.2 km) high, where it rendezvoused with *Cosmos 967*, sent up earlier. After making four orbits alongside its target, *Cosmos 970* moved far enough away to prevent damage to *Cosmos 967* and exploded like a giant hand grenade. With this mission, the Russians clearly demonstrated the capability, refined from earlier flights, of destroying one satellite in space with another.

Today, the Soviet killer-satellite system consists of a

number of large craft launched into orbit by SS-9 booster rockets. The satellites use a combination of infrared and radar tracking to approach a target; then a conventional explosive charge is detonated, destroying both the killer satellite itself and the target.

Most tests have required only a single orbit to perform the intercept. This technique reduces the defender's ability to track the attacker and respond in time. Although generally tested in low orbits, up to approximately 600 miles (960 km), at least one Russian killer satellite flew as high as 1,200 to 1,300 miles (1,920 to 2,080 km) above the earth—an altitude that would reach most current U.S. surveillance and navigational spacecraft. Although Soviet killer satellites cannot yet reach U.S. communications and early-warning craft in geosynchronous orbit 22,300 miles (35,680 km) up, military officials believe that during the next few years the Russians will achieve this capability, too, through the use of a large booster. In addition, although it is believed that the Soviet system is armed with conventional warheads, nuclear weapons could be carried, significantly increasing each satellite's kill radius.

In February 1982, the U.S. Joint Chiefs of Staff issued a report to Congress declaring that they believed the Soviets have already developed a system that has the potential to destroy satellites in high orbits.[16] Earlier, then Defense Secretary Caspar Weinberger has stated that "it is anticipated the Soviets will continue work in this area with a goal of negating satellites in high orbit."

Four months later, Weinberger's prophecy proved chillingly accurate. On June 18, 1982, the Russians orchestrated the launchings of two intercontinental ballistic missiles, two antiballistic missiles, one submarine-launched ballistic missile, two military satellites, one SS-20 intermediate range ballistic missile, and one killer satellite.

Military experts who analyzed this exercise concluded that the Soviets were fighting an imaginary nuclear war. The first step was the launch of the killer satellite to simulate the blinding of U.S. surveillance satellites in space. The ICBMs were launched in a mock attack on U.S. land-based missile sites with a second strike aimed at U.S. cities. The ABMs were used to practice shooting down counterattacking U.S. missiles. All the firings were coordinated under a unified Soviet command and control network.

Meanwhile, the U.S. position on killer satellites has been curiously inconsistent through the years. The United States pioneered the development of antisatellite weapons as far back as the early 1960s, through a program called Project Saint. But this was dropped when defense officials concluded that such a weapon was not needed.

Little was done in the early 1970s, when the Russian testing program was dormant. But when the Soviets began testing again in the 1976–77 period, President Gerald R. Ford ordered the rapid deployment of a new American killer satellite that would be "a bit more sophisticated" than the Russian version.

However, soon after President Jimmy Carter took office in 1977, another policy change was ordered. Defense budgets in general were slashed, and the United States followed a commitment to "maximize pacification" of space. President Carter ordered a new study of the situation and put a cap on American killer-satellite spending, limiting work to the development of the technology only.

But as the Russians continued their testing with obviously improved and highly maneuverable models of a killer satellite, the Carter administration reversed itself. The result was a presidential directive (PD-37) in June 1978 which stated in essence that the United States would conduct activities in space necessary to the support of such functions as navigations, command and control, communications, early warning, and surveillance and space defense. The directive proposed three areas of action:

- enhancing the survivability of space systems;
- initiating bilateral discussions with the Soviet Union on limiting weapons in space;
- and, in the absence of an agreement on antisatellites, developing a U.S. antisatellite capability.

Said Harold Brown, President Carter's secretary of defense: "The Soviets currently possess an operational antisatellite system which could be used to attack some U.S. satellites. We certainly have no desire to engage in a space-weapons race. However, the Soviets, with their present capability, are leaving us with little choice. Because of our growing dependence on space systems, we can hardly permit them to have a dominant position in ASAT. We might have to take steps to deter attacks on our satellites and to have the capability to destroy Soviet satellites if necessary."

Work was begun on development of a U.S. system of killer satellites. The first satellite to be developed out of this program was a miniature vehicle consisting of a cylinder only 2.5 feet (0.75 m) long and 1.5 feet (0.45 m) across, ringed with small rockets. It weighs just 35 pounds (15.75 kg). For an attack on satellites in low orbit altitudes, the miniature interceptor would be launched into space by heavily modified variations of such missiles as the Shirke or SRAM, which in turn would be fired from F-15 aircraft. The tiny killer satellite would hunt its prey using infrared (heat-seeking) sensors and an onboard computer. It would destroy satellites merely by impact, without explosives. Impact speeds would range from 10,000 to 40,000 feet (3,000 to 12,000 m) per second, depending on the altitude and location of the satellite to be attacked.

For intercept-and-destroy missions at high orbital altitudes, the ASAT would be launched by a space booster, or perhaps eventually from the space shuttle. Because of its small size, which enables it to be maneuvered easily, the U.S. ASAT will be a more capable weapon than its Soviet counterpart. Since it will be launched into space by an F-15 aircraft, it can be based anywhere F-15s fly, presumably even aboard aircraft carriers. The Russian system is sent into space by land-based rockets requiring elaborate launch facilities.

The air force is also working on more advanced systems. One version would use an even more maneuverable satellite and a powerful infrared sensor to seek out enemy satellites over great distances. Another possibility is the placement of armed mines in space near targets which would explode on command.

"These alternate approaches will provide a mixed force that will complicate Soviet defense and exploit new technology," says Lieutenant General Thomas B. Stafford, the air force's deputy chief of staff for Research, Development, and Acquisition.

It is possible that the U.S. system might someday be capable of stopping a Soviet ASAT enroute to its target, although the single-orbit attack profile of a Russian killer satellite would make attack warning, assessment of the situation, and response timing very difficult problems. It is believed that on at least three separate occasions, for example, Russian killer satellites have passed close to American satellites in orbit and then moved on, leaving almost no time for analysis or response.

Consequently, the Department of Defense has recently become deeply concerned about the survivability of satellites in space. For the last few years it has commissioned studies and developmental work designed to protect such objects from enemy attack.

Until recently, few satellites have been built for survival against weapons systems. Most of those now orbiting the earth could easily be knocked out. Many are stationary, and others are comparatively slow moving. They make for easy targets. Most are thin-skinned and unarmed—hence very vulnerable.

When the Soviets began retesting their antisatellite system in 1976, however, the U.S. Air Force began experimenting with "armored" spacecraft. Two survivable communications satellites, *LES-8* and *LES-9*, were launched in an effort to demonstrate an effective means of hardening satellites against possible nuclear- and conventional-weapons blasts.

Special features included circuitry protected by radiation shielding and an extremely low-drift, single-axis gyroscope for altitude control to eliminate dependence on external sensors, which are more vulnerable to nuclear effects. The two satellites were powered by nuclear generators instead of solar cells. (Solar cells are more vulnerable to damage from explosion).

The United States is also looking at a number of other programs to protect satellites. Among them are

- making satellites more maneuverable so they can take evasive action if threatened. It may be possible, for instance, to "train" a satellite to sense the approach of a hostile spacecraft and "jump" orbits to avoid the pursuer;
- covering satellites with mirrors or heat shields that would enable the satellite to deflect or absorb blast effects:
- launching "dark satellites"—orbiters whose systems would be dormant, making them difficult to detect. These craft would be activated only to replace a satellite that had been destroyed;
- placing satellites in higher orbits, where they would be more difficult to track and destroy. It would take, for example, several hours for a killer satellite or a smart bullet to climb 22,300 miles

(35,680 km) to the altitude of a geosynchronous satellite;

- placing key satellites in orbits halfway to the moon, which would take an enemy's killer vehicles twelve to twenty hours to reach;
- launching satellite "decoys" to lure attacking spacecraft from the main targets;
- having standby satellites ready for launching on a moment's notice to replace any disabled payloads in space;
- doubling up on the missions of satellites by putting military sensors on nonmilitary spacecraft;
- developing a system for satellites that could sound one alarm if they are approached by an enemy craft and another if they come under attack; and
- arming satellites with retaliatory weapons, which could fire on enemy satellites if they draw too close in orbit.

Also being considered are better ways of protecting the ground stations that control the satellites. One proposal calls for development of a network of trailer stations, which could move around the country during time of attack, making them hard to detect.

Each of these programs complicates satellite launchings and flights. In addition, more powerful launch vehicles would be needed to hoist heavier, armored satellites into orbit. And the question remains: How much armor is needed for protection? Some claim it is not hard to imagine the launching into space of a satellite the size of a beach ball cocooned in layers of armor the size of a Sherman tank.

The space shuttle can be used to improve the survivability of satellites. It is capable of carrying heavier payloads and can also place a number of satellites in orbit on one trip. But the shuttle itself could be a prime target should an enemy wish to initiate aggression high above the earth. It is relatively slow moving and lacks the maneuverability of the smaller, swifter killer satellites. Some critics of the shuttle call it a sitting duck in orbit. And present plans call for the United States to build only four shuttle orbiter systems. The destruction of just one or two of these would severely cripple America's space program.

For these reasons it appears likely that the most important mission of any American killler-satellite system will be to deter Soviet use of killer satellites. This mission is particularly important considering that the United States relies more heavily than the Soviets do on satellites for its military communications. Most of the Soviet Union's critical communications are land-based and restricted to Eastern Europe or to the Asian land-mass.

The United States is becoming increasingly reliant on satellites for ship and aerial navigation as well. One expert analyst has suggested that the Russians might use their ASATs to eliminate U.S. surveillance satellites and disrupt command communications in case of a breakout of nonnuclear hostilities between Warsaw Pact nations and members of the North Atlantic Treaty Organization in Europe.

In any case, the consequences of destroying a satellite belonging to either side would be very grim indeed. Says one military expert: "In my opinion, you are at war when one country shoots down another country's satellites. The Soviets could not be sure how we would respond—by shooting down one of their satellites, by sinking one of their warships, or by destroying Moscow."

Strangely, the Russians have never admitted that they have a killer satellite program, and, in fact, have been highly critical of any efforts made in this area by the United States. In April 1983, for example, the head of the

Soviet delegation to the United Nation's Conference on Disarmament, Viktor Israelyan, said: "The orbiting of antisatellite systems or any other types of weapons would inevitably have an extreme destabilizing effect on the international situation, and the danger of war—a nuclear, all-destructive war threatening the whole of mankind—would sharply grow."

In December 1983, Radio Moscow said, "Tests of a new satellite killer . . . would be the first United States step toward extending the arms race into space. It would be naive to believe that a powerful nation such as the Soviet Union, the pioneer in space exploration, would allow the United States to achieve military supremacy in space."

U.S. officials find this attitude and the Soviet denial of developing such a system themselves puzzling to say

In April, 1986, in an experiment at White Sands Missile Range, New Mexico, the U.S. Army launched a 12-foot (3.6-m) long hypersonic flight vehicle which was guided by built-in homing radar towards an aluminum sphere 44 inches (112 cm) in diameter. The sphere was suspended 3,000 feet (914 m) below a large helium-filled balloon positioned at 15,000 feet (5,000 m) altitude. The target was destroyed. The experiment was conducted under the auspices of the Strategic Defense Initiative Organization to verify that nonnuclear intercept of missiles within the atmosphere was achievable.

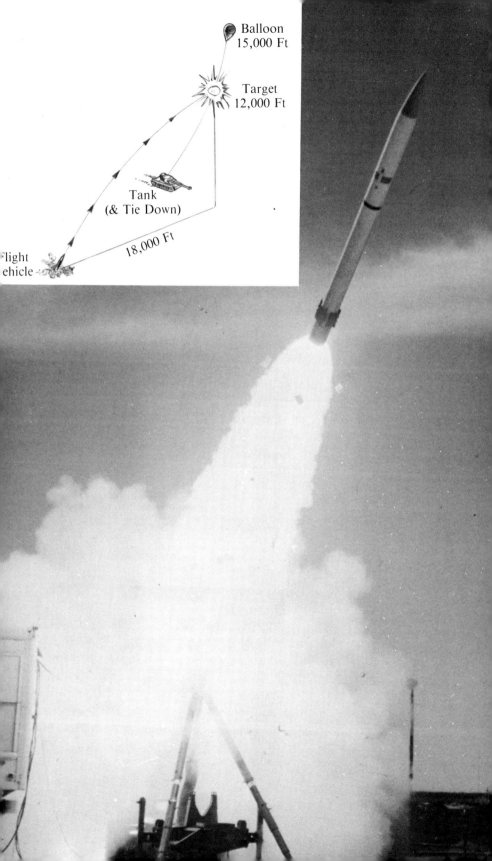

Balloon
15,000 Ft

Target
12,000 Ft

Tank
(& Tie Down)

18,000 Ft

Flight
Vehicle

the least. This is especially true in light of the fact that the Russians have been working hard in recent years to upgrade their system. They have been concentrating on finding new techniques for quick fueling and launching of their killer satellites, and, according to U.S. experts, have reached the point where they can get a rocket bearing a killer satellite loaded with fuel and ready to launch in ninety minutes. Such a quick reaction system permits an attack on an enemy satellite without a lengthy pursuit in orbit. On at least two occasions, a Soviet killer satellite had been seen to come up from below and make its kill in a matter of minutes, before it has orbited the earth once.

The United States also has made a number of refinements in its program in recent years. On September 30, 1986, the air force announced it had successfully tested the infrared guidance system on its antisatellite missile during a flight over the Pacific Ocean off California.

Previously, in September 1985, an antisatellite was fired into space, where it tracked and destroyed an aging research satellite. However, following that test, the U.S. Congress banned further experiments involving the destruction of objects in orbit.

This particular killer satellite vehicle is a two-stage rocket designed to be carried to a high altitude by an F-15 aircraft and then launched into space. The missile is loaded with sophisticated sensors that allow it to guide itself to targets in low earth orbit. Its "warhead" does not contain any explosives. The missile destroys its target through impact only.

The Reagan administration has contested the Congressional ban on testing in space, arguing the Soviets already have a workable antisatellite missile of their own. The Soviets have been observing a voluntary moratorium on further testing of that rocket, however, and Congress has proposed extending the ban. The matter had not been resolved at the time this book went to press.

But whether or not further testing is allowed, and regardless of whether the Russians will continue to refine their system, this appears to be yet another arena of weaponry where both the United States and Russia either have now, or can develop soon, the capability to kill each other's satellites in space. It is to be hoped that, if this is realized, neither country will be the first to strike such a blow, knowing that the attacked nation can respond in kind.

N I N E T E E N

COMMAND POSTS IN SPACE

To date, the major thrust of U.S. military activity in space has been in the area of unmanned vehicles. Computerized robots perform a variety of critical defense functions in orbit, including communications, meteorology, early warning of enemy attack, surveillance, and navigation. Likewise, future concepts, such as the development of a killer satellite and the positioning of defensive laser weapons systems in space, also call for unmanned vehicles. A growing number of military experts, however, are becoming increasingly concerned about the fact that the United States does not appear to have any definite plans for establishing manned bases in orbit, while the Soviets are fast developing such capabilities.

Some air force officials would like to see America's global strike force controlled from a manned command post in space. One spokesman, for example, has said: "We may find that this is the only survivable command and control structure. Should such a spaceborne command post become necessary, it would have to be large enough to carry all the electronic gear required to gather, process, and disseminate operational information on a global basis. It would have to be capable of defending itself against any interference or attacks from the ground or in space." He added that such a station would have to be able to dispatch manned ships to protect against attacks and to search out suspected enemy weapons carriers in space, board them, and, if necessary, neutralize them.

Says Lieutenant General J.F. O'Malley, deputy chief of staff of Air Force Operations, Plans and Readiness: "I feel an undefinable but very real sense of urgency—a basic premonition that in some future period of time we are going to look back and wonder why we were so slow to comprehend the value of man in space. In contrast, the Soviets have an aggressive man-in-space program— one which they apparently believe is paying enough dividends to warrant the steadily increasing cost. I fervently hope the advent of the shuttle will regain the initiative for the United States in employing man in space."

The shuttle, however, was not designed nor does it have the capability to be a permanent station in space. It was designed to ferry payloads into low earth orbit. The shuttle can currently stay in orbit for only about seven to ten days. At a later point this may be extended for periods of up to sixty or ninety days. But the shuttle was not designed to stay in space indefinitely.

Technologically, the United States has the expertise to build permanent or semipermanent manned stations in earth orbit. The air force has had a strong interest in developing such a capability for nearly twenty years. However, its two experimental programs for building such a station—the X20 Dyna-Soar program and the Manned Orbiting Laboratory—were both killed in the 1960s, largely because of the huge expenses involved.

The United States did prove, however, through NASA's Skylab program in the early 1970s, that people could survive and function well in space for reasonable periods of time. Skylab was actually a temporary space station. It consisted of a remodeled third stage—a huge cylindrical shell 48 feet (14.4 m) long and 21 feet (6.3 m) in diameter—of a Saturn V moon rocket.

Skylab was about the size of a small three-bedroom

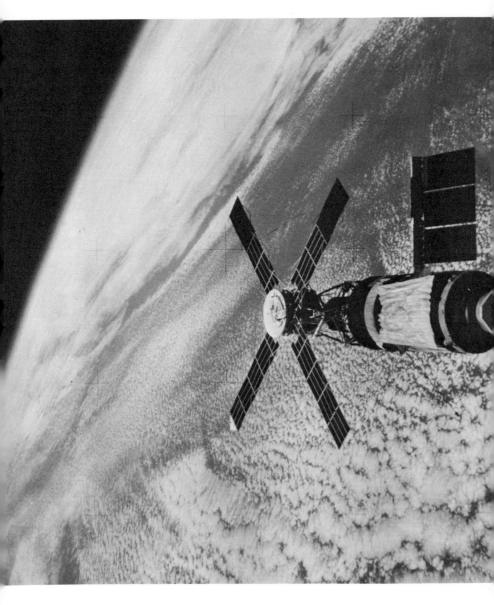

*The success of Skylab, a temporary space station,
proved that human beings could live and work safely,
comfortably, and effectively in space.*

house. Grid-pattern floors and ceilings were installed in the tank, separating the living and working areas into a two-story arrangement. In the tail end of the cylinder, solid partitions were designed to divide the crew's living quarters into separate sleeping compartments, a dining area, a bathroom, and an office station. The other end of Skylab, covering about three quarters of the total space, was outfitted as a large laboratory where most of the experimental work was to be done.

Three separate teams of astronauts lived and worked in Skylab at different times. Each was launched from the earth in a modified Apollo spacecraft, similar to the ones that carried astronauts to the moon. In each case the craft docked with Skylab about 230 miles (370 km) above the earth. The crew entered and left the huge tank through an airlock module. The astronauts returned to earth in the Apollo spacecraft in the same way as all previous U.S. manned space flights had—by the capsule's reentering the earth's atmosphere and splashing down in the ocean.

The first crew remained on the station for four weeks, the second for fifty-nine days, and the third for eighty-four days. During each period, the astronauts performed a number of scientific experiments. Doctors were extremely pleased by the astronauts' excellent physical condition when they returned home.

Skylab proved that human beings could live and work safely, comfortably, and effectively in near-zero gravity conditions for at least short periods of time. Not only that, but the astronauts did a number of things that could not have been done by robots, further proving the value of humans in space.

When Skylab was launched into orbit May 14, 1973, two solar panels failed to deploy as planned. The problem was critical. Without the use of these panels, which converted sunlight to electricity, Skylab's electrical capacity was cut in half. And without the panels to protect it from the sun, the station's metal hull heated up to nearly 300° F. (149° C.) during Skylab's first day in orbit. The interior of the tank, where the astronauts were to live, became unbearably hot, with an average temperature of 120° F. (49° C.).

Officials feared that the intense heat would spoil food and damage medicines and photographic film aboard the craft. Some feared that the entire $2.5-billion Skylab program would be lost almost before it had begun. But engineers devised a protective aluminized awning to shade the station. Then the astronaut team of Charles Conrad, Paul Weitz, and Joseph Kerwin was launched into space. There, they successfully opened the makeshift sunshade and later snapped off a jammed bolt, freeing one of the stuck solar panels. This effectively lowered the interior tank temperatures and provided the needed additional electrical power to complete the mission. It also demonstrated people's ability to improvise and to work well in a weightless environment.

But following the return of the last astronaut team early in 1974, Skylab was abandoned. Years later its speed slowed, and it fell out of its orbit. The giant tank then reentered the earth's atmosphere, and most of it disintegrated before it reached the earth's surface in Australia's backcountry. And except for one cooperative manned mission with the Soviet Union in 1975—Apollo-Soyuz—in which United States and Soviet spacemen rendezvoused in orbit and flew together for a brief period, the United States did not put another person into space until the first shuttle test flight in April 1981.

The Soviets, in contrast, have been extremely active in their manned flight programs and have built a station capability that is now years ahead of anything the United States developed. In fact, the Soviets pioneered the space station concept nearly two years before Skylab.

On June 7, 1971, cosmonauts Georgi Dobrovolsky, Vladislav Volkov, and Viktor Patsayev maneuvered their Soyuz spacecraft to a rendezvous and docking with the Salyut station, which had been launched into orbit seven weeks earlier. The first Salyut was smaller than Skylab—about the size of an average house trailer—and the cosmonauts lived aboard it for twenty-three days, suffering no apparent ill effects from their stay in space.

The Soyuz flight ended in tragedy, however. On the spacecraft's trip back to earth, air somehow escaped from the capsule, and the cosmonauts died of embolism, caused by air bubbles in the blood.

This did not deter the Soviets from their efforts. In 1977, they launched Salyut 6 into orbit. A 21-ton vehicle with two docking ports, the manned space station was periodically resupplied by an unmanned Progress cargo craft that carried fuel, water, food, and supplies and used its engines to adjust Salyut's slowly decaying orbit. Several teams of cosmonauts lived on Salyut 6 for varying periods of time, until it fell out of orbit in July 1982 and burned up in the atmosphere. Anatoly Berezovoy and Valetin Lebedey hold the record—237 days in space, aboard Salyut 7.

Since the first orbital flight of Yuri Gagarin, in 1961, the Soviets have placed fifty cosmonauts into orbit on a total of forty-seven missions. The United States, over the same time span, has sent forty-five astronauts on thirty-three missions in space. All American flights, however, except for the three Skylab missions, were of very short duration—only a few days. By contrast, Soviet cosmonauts have logged a total of five and a half years in orbit, most on Salyut stations.

And although the Soviets claim to fly every flight in the name of science, U.S. intelligence sources say that in reality at least two early Salyuts were military stations and that a good part of the cosmonauts' "civilian" work had a strong military cast. It is known, for example, that Salyut 6 served as the testbed in space for an astronomical telescope camera and an earth-observation camera. Both were later moved to a surveillance satellite. A special furnace on Salyut was used to forge new metal alloys vital for sophisticated reconnaissance hardware. Some cosmonauts also worked on perfecting navigational tracking and early-warning systems while aboard the station.

With much greater experience in manned orbital flight, the Soviets have uncovered some physical problems that result from long stays in a nearly weightless environment. Muscles deteriorate despite daily exercise programs. The heart changes its pattern of contractions. Bones lose up to one half of one percent of their calcium every month because new deposits require the pull of gravity, which is nearly absent in space. Then there are the mental and psychological effects of spending a lot of time without the company of the opposite sex.

Nevertheless, the Soviets are believed to be developing plans for newer and larger space stations. This has some high-ranking U.S. military officials very worried. Says Lieutenant General Stafford, himself a former astronaut: "I am concerned that they [the Soviets] may be developing a manned space capability about which we know very little. They understand the force enhancement available from space and have devoted considerable effort to the development of space systems."

One aspect of the Soviet's manned military space program that is of particular concern to U.S. experts is that the Soviets seem well on the way toward placing a manned command and control spacecraft in orbit that could perform along the lines of the U.S. E-4B National Emergency Airborne Command Post. Such a capability, say these experts, combined with America's continued reliance on unmanned and more vulnerable satellites, could severely handicap this country in the event of a strategic nuclear war. With a person in space commanding the assault of killer satellites upon U.S. satellites, for example, the Soviets might be able to knock out communications, weather, navigational, surveillance, and early-warning systems so crucial to American defense.

United States government sources believe the Soviets are now working on plans to build a twelve-person space station. They also say the Soviets are developing a winged, reusable space vehicle, similar to the shuttle, which would be launched to service the station from a surface ship in the Caspian or Aral seas.

Sources also say that the Soviets themselves have talked about space stations in the late 1980s that would be permanently staffed by ten to twenty-five cosmonauts at a time, or even larger Salyuts in the 1990s with crews of up to 120 men and women. Such stations would presumably be assembled in orbit out of separate modules ferried from earth and would function in orbit for years.

Some military experts envision mammoth American military installations in space by the year 2000. They see elaborate communications facilities, sophisticated observation systems, and workshops for repair, refueling, and rearming of space battleships. A single installation might support a space fleet spread out thousands of miles in space, perhaps extending as far as the near planets, poised and ready to fight a space war. Such an outpost might also become a command center for the president of the United States in case of war.

"Whether we'll see such an installation is something we can't foresee right now," one defense planner has said. "But who knows what lies ahead? Man has moved from the earth's atmosphere into space in an instant of time. We who have witnessed this scientific miracle must acknowledge that it could lead to developments that we cannot now define."

T W E N T Y

BENEFITS OR BATTLEFIELDS?

Will space become the next great battleground, a vast arena in which super battle stations equipped with weapons of awesome firepower and accuracy constantly patrol, ready to unleash their destructive force on an instant's notice? Or will space be used, as both the United States and the Soviet Union have repeatedly declared throughout the years, exclusively for peaceful purposes?

If future wars are fought, will they be waged in orbit, high above the earth, leaving this planet as the garden spot of the universe? Will nuclear war on earth become an empty threat once defensive laser weapons systems become operational, standing silent guard over the world, primed to knock down any ICBM seconds after its launch? Will the world's superpowers somehow find a way to meet at the negotiating tables and declare a halt to the costly spatial-weapons race?

The answers to these and dozens of other crucial questions still lie at some point in the future. Meanwhile, the arguments, pro and con, wage on as to whether the United States should continue to build a large-scale military capability in space. Both sides command compelling arguments.

Those who are in favor of constructing and maintaining a strong defense buildup, both on earth and in space, argue that if the United States does not do this, it will become a second-rate power and eventually will be subject to Soviet nuclear blackmail threats. President Reagan's former secretary of defense, Caspar Weinberger, for example, has warned that the Soviets are "engaged in the greatest buildup of military power seen in modern times." He warns that nations falling behind in this race for military equality "may reach such a level of unpreparedness that they will become afraid to redress the situation for fear of provoking the conflict they are seeking to prevent."

Dr. William J. Perry, a former under secretary of defense for Research and Engineering, reported in 1983 to Congress that the Soviet Union was out-investing the United States in military expenditures by a margin of about two to one. He said that over the past ten years, the Soviet Union has spent $350 billion more on its military and defense programs than the United States has. He also reported that the Soviet Union is outproducing this country by more than two to one in most categories of military equipment.

He added the following: "The Soviet Union now has about twice as great an effort as we have in military research and development, creating a growing risk of technological surprise." To this point, Lieutenant General Richard C. Henry, commander of the Air Force Systems Command's Space Division, says: "The Soviets are graduating 300,000 engineers each year compared to our 50,000."

Some experts also point out that the Russians are outspending and outperforming the United States in military space programs. A congressional report on United States and Soviet progress in space, for example, stated: "About 56 percent of U.S. space flights are conducted for the Department of Defense, with 48 percent strictly for military purposes. About 69 percent of Soviet flights are for strictly military purposes.[17]

"About 48 percent of current U.S. space funds are spent for the programs of the Department of Defense, which are less expensive than those of NASA because more of them are for routine operations than new development," the report continued. "Corresponding breakdowns for the Soviet total program are harder to establish because of their secrecy of budget data, and their claim that all flights are scientific. Yet a very considerable number of their flights give convincing indications of serving military purposes."

Those who oppose development of orbital weapons systems contend that such action will lead only to a continued escalation of the nuclear arms race, extending it to the vastness of space. They claim that Americans are being misled by those who claim that the Soviet Union is now militarily stronger than the United States. They say that in any case the United States already has a military arsenal powerful enough to deter any enemy attack, now or in the foreseeable future.

Former Secretary of Defense Harold Brown has addressed some of these points: "Some have said that the Soviet Union has already achieved military superiority over the United States. These voices speak only of American weaknesses and Soviet strengths. They would have us—and others—believe that we are weaker than, in fact, we are.

"The truth is that we are second to none. Our military power, coupled with that of our allies, is not exceeded by any combination of nations on earth. Our strengths are abundant, if occasionally ignored by some. Our technological prowess is the envy of every military power, and we will continue to exploit it to our advantage.

"Some have promised American military superiority over the Soviet Union," Brown said. "The truth is that comprehensive military superiority for either side—

absolute supremacy, if you will—is a military and economic impossibility—if the other [side] is determined to prevent it. There can be no return to the days of the American nuclear monopoly. There can be no winner in an all-out arms race."

Opponents of extending the arms race into space are deeply concerned that an increase in weapons development will eventually lead to a disastrous war, either through error or, as Paul C. Warnke put it, through fear. Warnke is a former director of the U.S. Arms Control and Disarmament Agency. He said: "As the weapons increase in number, sophistication, and accuracy, each side has to think of something inevitable.

"At some point, when the weapons are so many and so accurate, each side may have to figure they have to strike first because neither side would have a chance to strike second. The issue is not between hard-liners and soft-liners. The bottom line is coexistence or no existence."

There are other arguments, too. Some fear that the buildup of weapons systems in space, especially of armed unmanned vehicles, increases the chances of poor and potentially fatal judgments. It is conceivable, they point out, that a battle station in orbit could attack a foreign missile or spacecraft in response to deceptive, incomplete, or even inaccurate data. For example, a Soviet decision to test decoy material or to launch a series of manned spacecraft simultaneously for a peaceful experiment might momentarily bewilder or deceive an American battle station into taking lethal, irretrievable action. Such an event would almost certainly trigger a cataclysmic U.S.–Soviet confrontation.

On the other hand, proponents of using space for defense purposes say that having military systems in space *lessens*, rather than *heightens*, the chances of a nuclear war starting by accident on earth. One congressional report said: "American analysts argue that such information [from reconnaissance satellites] from space

– 129

is one of the greatest safeguards against miscalculation by the major powers, and, hence, in the absence of explicit international agreements for open skies and ground inspection, is the best bargain all countries of the world have to limit the arms race and to provide insurance against a general holocaust of thermonuclear arms."

The report also indicated that it was a good thing the Soviets, too, had military systems in space. It said: "There is no doubt that the Soviet Union has a large and regular program of military support flights, including use of satellites for photographic observation, electronic listening, weather reporting, communications relaying, and ships' navigation.

"Although these space services undoubtedly enhance Soviet military capabilities, in net balance they probably are to the advantage of the United States if surer knowledge between these two big powers makes each more cautious and less prone to error in estimates."

Another point of contention among those who favor developing weapons systems in space and those who don't concerns how such weapons might be used. There are those, for instance, who are convinced that the battleground of the future will not be on earth but in orbit. They say that space is the ideal site for fighting—that it will provide the battlefields in a time when arms and war have outgrown the planet. This way, our civilization will be preserved. Nuclear weapons could explode in orbit, for instance, without danger to the human race and the delicate earth below. The solar wind would harmlessly disperse the radioactive fallout.

But others say that this view is too simplistic and unrealistic. They say that active military capabilities in space require the introduction of lethal weapons and that this increases the possibility of combat breaking out both in and from space. The potential for space-related warfare includes not simply space-to-space warfare, but earth-to-earth and space-to-earth warfare as well. It also clearly signals the end of that period in which space could be assumed to be a sanctuary, or military-free zone.

Still another group of experts believes that the deployment of advanced weapons systems in space is the *only* way to assure peace on earth. Senator Wallop of Wyoming is the chief congressional exponent of this view.

Over the past decade and a half the United States has been developing weapons that are offensive in nature. That is, they are designed strictly to inflict damage upon an enemy's society.

American policy has been based on the assumption that any nuclear exchange would be so disastrous that neither the United States nor the Soviet Union would be willing to take the risk of trying to come out in "better" shape than the other. This illusion of "Mutual Assured Destruction" has blinded U.S. policymakers to the need for a potent defensive system.

President Reagan has indicated that one of his top priorities is to accelerate development of a modern defensive weapon—a space-based laser that could be used to defend against ballistic missiles launched from the Soviet Union. This system holds the potential of moving us away from the brink of nuclear war that we are presently standing on.

"Several dozen laser weapons systems deployed in space would revolutionize the strategic balance as we have known it for two decades—most importantly by tipping the balance of modern warfare in favor of defense, thereby lessening the potential destructive effects of war."

To this point, Harrison Schmitt of New Mexico, a former astronaut, and Senator William Roth of Delaware add: "The United States needs a new strategic policy for the rest of this century, not continued reliance upon a doctrine based on weapons of mass destruction. We must take advantage of America's technological superiority to leapfrog the Soviet Union and develop strategic weapons that will make weapons of mass destruction obsolete."

And, finally, the argument persists as to whether or not Star Wars is a practical concept that can be developed within a reasonable amount of time for a reasonable amount of money. Despite some technical breakthroughs in recent years, there still is a cadre of knowledgeable experts who believe a real Star Wars defense system in space is at best decades and hundreds of billions of dollars away from reality. And, at worst, they say, even if it ever can be developed, it will not be effective.

Representative of this view is the Union of Concerned Scientists, a private group. A committee report from this group has stated: "Total ballistic missile defense—the protection of American society against the full weight of a Soviet nuclear attack—is unattainable if the Soviet Union exploits the many vulnerabilities intrinsic to all the schemes that have been proposed so far."[18]

Proponents of Star Wars counter that recent successes in using "off-the-shelf" technology to shoot down intercontinental ballistic missile warheads in space makes it hard to make the case that "it can't be done," or that a successful defense will take decades of research and a trillion dollars to complete.

While these arguments rage on, the Reagan administration continues to pursue its policy of building up the national defense. As federal government budgets for social welfare and other civilian programs are being cut, the defense budget is being increased. It appears that the Soviet Union, too, is giving top priority status to a continued buildup of its military programs.

In light of these recent trends, a growing number of experts see the arming of space as inevitable. One who does is Dr. James Van Allen of the University of Iowa, the prominent space scientist for whom the radiation belts surrounding the earth were named after he detected them, using data from the first American satellite.

"The military use of the shuttle is going to be dominant, while civil uses will be minor," he declares. "NASA is going to be trampled to death by the Defense Department on shuttle use, so why not be honest about it and call it a military program?"

Said Major General William R. Yost, former director of Air Space Systems, Control, and Communications for the air force: "I firmly believe that in the next two decades, the military use of space will have gained the kind of acceptance we accord to airplanes today."

Adds Lieutenant General O'Malley: "I believe the use of space by military forces is at a point similar to the position of air power after World War I. While there are undoubtedly well-intentioned people who decry what they regard as the potential for militarization of a pristine frontier, history teaches us that each time a new medium is opened to man it is exploited to gain a military advantage."

"Our overall game plan is not to permit the other side [the Soviet Union] to attain unilateral superiority in space," says a top national security official. "There are two ways to do it. One is to build up our capability until it is at least equivalent. The other is to get him [the Soviets] to get rid of some of his capability [disarmament]. Either one is acceptable to us."

For now, both of these courses of action are being pursued. Although there is the continuing hope of bringing the United States and the Soviet Union back to the negotiating tables for meaningful talks on arms reductions on earth and weapons bans in space, the Reagan administration also believes that it must prepare for the worst in case such talks never materialize or prove fruitless. To Reagan this means the United States must build military systems to neutralize those being developed by the Soviets, systems designed for use both on earth and in space.

And so, the paradox persists. Scientists call space the greatest potential frontier, with limitless resources and opportunities for people. Will it be used for the benefit and growth of all earth's creatures, ushering in an era of human prosperity for centuries to come? Or will it instead become the ultimate battleground, a vast arena for the release of human hostilities and the unleashing of superweapons that could conceivably destroy our entire planet? The decisions being made and developments under way today may well provide the answers not only to these questions but also tell us the future course and direction of human civilization.

NOTES

Chapter 1
1. Robert Jastrow, "Why We Need Star Wars," *Reader's Digest*, February 1985.

Chapter 2
2. *Science News*, April 2, 1983.

Chapter 3
3. Janet Raloff, "Beam Weapons: Department of Defense's High Tech Gamble," *Science News*, July 14, 1984.

Chapter 4
4. Edward Edelson, "Space Weapons: The Science Behind the Big Debate," *Popular Science*, July 1984.
5. "Department of Defense High Energy Laser Program." Fact sheet.
6. Senator Malcolm Wallop's Weekly Column, January 5, 1981. U.S. Senate, Washington, D.C.

Chapter 5
7. Brian Beckett, *Weapons of Tomorrow* (New York: Plenum Press, 1983).

8. "Space Based Weapons," *Newport News Daily Press*, October 19, 1986.

Chapter 6
9. Robert Jastrow, *How to Make Nuclear Weapons Obsolete* (Boston: Little, Brown, 1985).

Chapter 8
10. Brian Beckett, *Weapons of Tomorrow.*

Chapter 12
11. "Navstar Global Position System." Fact sheet.

Chapter 14
12. L.B. Taylor, *Space Shuttle* (New York: Crowell, 1979).
13. __*For All Mankind.* (New York: Dutton, 1974).

Chapter 17
14. Robert Jastrow, *How to Make Nuclear Weapons Obsolete.*
15. "How to Decide about Strategic Defense," *National Review*, January 31, 1986.

Chapter 18
16. "Space Weapons," *Science Digest*, April 1984.

Chapter 20
17. "How to Decide about Strategic Defense."
18. Edward Edelson, "Space Weapons: the Science Behind the Big Debate."

BIBLIOGRAPHY

Books

Beckett, Brian. *Weapons of Tomorrow.* New York: Plenum Press, 1983.

Broad, William J. *Star Warriors.* New York: Simon & Schuster, 1985.

Jastrow, Robert. *How to Make Nuclear Weapons Obsolete.* Boston: Little Brown and Company, 1985.

Oberg, James. *Red Star in Orbit: The Inside Story of Soviet Failure and Triumphs in Space.* New York: Random House, 1981.

Stockton, William, and John Noble Wilford. *Spaceliner: Report on the Columbia's Voyage.* New York: New York Times Press, 1981.

Taylor, LB., Jr. *For All Mankind: America's Space Programs of the Seventies and Beyond.* New York: E.P. Dutton, 1974.

_____. *The Nuclear Arms Race.* New York: Franklin Watts, 1982.

_____. *Space Shuttle.* New York: Thomas Y. Crowell, 1979.

Magazine Articles

"Additional Warning Satellites Expected," *Aviation Week & Space Technology* (May 14, 1973).

"Advanced Technology in Space," *Air Force Magazine* (June, 1981).

"Beam Weapons: DOD'S High Tech Gamble," *Science News* (July 14, 1984).

"Beyond the Balance of Terror," *Business Week* (November 19, 1984).

"Can Space Shuttle Fill the Air Force Bill?" *Air Force Magazine* (June 1981).

"Dachas in the Sky," *Newsweek* (April 27, 1981)

"Defense Technology: Moving into Space," *Air Force Magazine* (June 1979).

"How to Decide about Strategic Defense," *National Review* (Jan. 31, 1986).

"How Vulnerable Are USAF Military Space Systems?" *Air Force Magazine* (June 1972).

"Missiles vs. Antimissiles," *America* (February 28, 1981).

"The New Military Race in Space," *Business Week* (June 4, 1979).

"Now a New Arms Race in Space," *Newsweek* (April 27, 1977).

"Now, Instant Warning if U.S. Is Attacked," *U.S. News & World Report* (November 15, 1971).

"Opportunities & Imperatives of Ballistic Missile Defense," *Strategic Review* (Fall 1979).

"Russia's Plot to Conquer the World," *Man's Magazine* (February 1973).

"A Space Age Arms Race," *Newsweek* (April 27 1981).

"Space Conflict Strategies," *Defense & Foreign Affairs* (August/September 1981).

"Space Shuttle Mired in Bureaucratic Feud," *Air Force Magazine* (September 1980).

"Space Wars," *Foreign Policy* (Fall 1981).

"Space Weapons," *Science Digest* (April 1984).

"Space Weapons—the Science Behind the Big Debate," *Popular Science* (July 1984).

"Spies in the Sky," *New York Times Magazine* (September 3, 1972).

"Star Wars Weapons May Come True," *U.S. News & World Report* (July 27, 1981).

"Text of Reagan Address on Defense Policy," *Congressional Quarterly* (March 26, 1983).

"Toward a New U.S. Strategy: Bold Strokes Rather Than Increments," *Strategic Review* (Spring 1981).

"War in Space: Good!" *New Scientist* (May 28, 1981).

"Why We Need 'Star Wars'," *Reader's Digest* (February 1985).

"Who Will Rule Space," *The Plain Truth* (June 1985).

Newspaper Articles

"Early Start of Talks on Satellites Urged," *New York Times* News Service (March 19, 1978).

"Military Strategy: Reagan Five-year Program," *Wall Street Journal* (February 8, 1982).

"Navigation Satellites Are Proving Useful to Many Users Besides the Military," *Wall Street Journal* (July 9, 1981).

"Put 'Star Wars' Before a Panel," *New York Times* (November 11, 1986).

"Reagan Says Soviet Barred Accord on Arms Reduction," *New York Times* (October 14, 1986).

"Robots and Rays May Have Role in Future U.S. Arsenal," *Los Angeles Times* (January 9, 1978).

"Satellite Killer Tested by Soviets," *New York Times* (January 28, 1972).

"Soviets Making Strides in Satellite-Killers," *Associated Press* (February 10, 1982).

"Space Wars," *Associated Press* (March 19, 1978).

"Space-based Weaponry," *Newport News Daily Press* (October 19, 1986).

"Star Guides Anti-Satellite Missile," *Newport News Daily Press* (October 1, 1986).

"Star Wars Proved Fatal in Iceland," *The Washington Post* (October 13, 1986).

"Star Wars Satellites Complete Test," *Newport News Daily Press* (AP) (September 6, 1986).

"Top 'Star Wars' Researchers Debate Weapons' Practicality," *Newport News Daily Press* (October 19, 1986).

"U.S. Russian Satellites Now Near 2,000," *Associated Press* (January 15, 1978).

"U.S. to Award 1st Contracts on Space Plane," *New York Times* (April 6, 1986).

Booklets, Pamphlets, Documents, and Bulletins

"Agreement Governing the Activities of States on the Moon and Other Celestial Bodies," UN General Assembly, December 14, 1979. UN Outer Space Affairs Division, New York, N.Y. 10017.

Issue Update—Senate Republican Conference, October 1981.

19th Annual Arms Control Report, U.S. Arms and Disarmament Agency, 1980. Washington, D.C. 20451.

"Pentagon Rebuts Charges of U.S. Military Weakness," *The Defense Monitor*, Vol. IX, Number 8A. Center for Defense Information, 600 Maryland Ave., SW, Washington, D.C. 20024.

Senator Malcolm Wallop's Weekly Column, January 5, 1981. U.S. Senate, Washington, D.C. 20330.

Other U.S. Air Force Fact Sheets:

"Our Role in Space"

"Navstar Global Positioning System"

"Defense Meteorological Satellite System"

"Department of Defense High Energy Laser Program"

(The four fact sheets above available from the Office of Public Information, Air Force Systems Command, Andrews Air Force Base, Maryland 20334.)

U.S. Navy Fact Sheet: "Transit." Department of the Navy, Office of Information, Washington, D.C.

U.S. Navy News Release, May 18, 1981: "NOVA Navigation Satellite." Department of the Navy, Office of Information, Washington, D.C.

Congressional Reports

"United States Civilian Space Policy" Report Prepared by the Subcommittee on Space Science and Applications, of the Committee on Science and Technology, U.S. House of Representatives, Ninety-seventh Congress, first session, April 1981. U.S. Government Printing Office, Washington, D.C.

"United States and Soviet Progress in Space: Summary Data Through 1979 and a Forward Look" Report prepared for the Subcommittee on Space Science and Applications, of the Committee on Science and Technology, U.S. House of Representatives, Ninety-seventh Congress, second session, April 1981. U.S. Government Printing Office, Washington, D.C.

INDEX